ADY - 4717
BS
475
.2

DATE DUE

WITHDRAWN

A LITERARY SURVEY
OF THE BIBLE

A
LITERARY SURVEY
OF THE BIBLE

by

JOYCE L. VEDRAL

Edited by Dennis Baker

LOGOS INTERNATIONAL
Plainfield, New Jersey

Unless otherwise indicated, all Scripture quotations are taken from the King James Version.

Library of Congress Catalog Card Number: 72-94184
International Standard Book Number: 0-88270-024-3
Copyright © 1973 by Logos International

Acknowledgments

I would like to thank our principal, Mrs. Sylvia Ballatt, for her words of encouragement as I pioneered this course. I am especially grateful to Dr. E. K. Friedman, A.P., English, for her guidance and support in the development of the Bible as Literature course in our school, which led to this book. I would also like to thank the teachers in the English department who by their interest and enthusiasm helped me to write this book.

Most of all, I thank my husband Charles Vedral for his steadfast encouragement, and my parents David and Martha Yellin for their continual interest and confidence.

Finally, I thank Mr. Dennis Baker, who labored over this manuscript, helping to put it into its final form.

" 'Remember me,' implored the Thief," by Emily Dickinson. Copyright 1914, 1942 by Martha Dickinson Bianchi, from *The Complete Poems of Emily Dickinson,* edited by Thomas H. Johnson, by permission of Little, Brown and Co.

" 'Remember me,' implored the Thief," "At least to pray is left, is left," "I took my power in my hand," by Emily Dickinson. Reprinted by permission of the publishers and the Trustees of Amherst College from Thomas H. Johnson, Editor, *The Poems of Emily Dickinson,* Cambridge, Mass.: The Belknap Press of Harvard University Press. Copyright 1951, by the President and Fellows of Harvard College.

"A Drizzling Easter Morning" and "In the Servants' Quarters" by Thomas Hardy. Reprinted with permission of Macmillan Publishing Co., Inc. from *Collected Poems* by Thomas Hardy. Copyright 1925 by The Macmillan Company. From *The Collected Poems of Thomas Hardy,* reprinted by permission of the Trustees of the Hardy Estate; Macmillan London & Basingstroke, and The Macmillan Company of Canada Limited.

"In the Valley of the Elwy" and "Thou art indeed just, Lord" by Gerard Manley Hopkins, reprinted by permission of Oxford University Press, by arrangement with the Society of Jesus.

"Christ in the Universe" by Alice Meynell, from *Later Poems* (1901) by permission of Charles Scribner's Sons.

"Easter Hymn" by A. E. Housman. From *The Collected Poems of A. E. Housman.* Copyright 1936 by Barclays Bank Ltd. Copyright © 1964 by Robert E. Symons. Reprinted by permission of Holt, Rinehart and Winston, Inc. and the Society of Authors as the literary representative of the Estate of A. E. Housman and Jonathan Cape Ltd., publishers of A. E. Housman's *Collected Poems.*

"The Carpenter's Son" by A. E. Housman. From "A Shropshire Lad" — Authorised Edition — from *The Collected Poems of A. E. Housman.* Copyright 1939, 1940, © 1965 by Holt, Rinehart and Winston, Inc. Copyright © 1967, 1968 by Robert E. Symons. Reprinted by permission of Holt, Rinehart and Winston and the Society of Authors as the literary representative of the Estate of A. E. Housman; and Jonathan Cape Ltd., publishers of A. E. Housman's *Collected Poems.*

"The Magi" by William Butler Yeats. Reprinted with permission of Macmillan Publishing Co., Inc. from *Collected Poems* by William Butler Yeats. Copyright 1916 by The Macmillan Company, renewed 1944 by Bertha Georgie Yeats. Reprinted also by permission of Mr. M. B. Yeats and The Macmillan Company of Canada Ltd. from *The Collected Poems of W. B. Yeats.*

"Bereft" by Robert Frost. From *The Poetry of Robert Frost* edited by Edward Connery Lathem. Copyright 1928, © 1969 by Holt, Rinehart and Winston, Inc. Copyright © 1956 by Robert Frost. Reprinted by permission of Holt, Rinehart and Winston, Inc.

"Ballad of the Goodly Fere" by Ezra Pound. From Ezra Pound, *Personae.* Copyright 1926 by Ezra Pound. Reprinted by permission of New Directions Publishing Corporation.

"Noah" by Siegfried Sassoon. From *Collected Poems* by Siegfried Sassoon. Copyright 1918 by E. P. Dutton Co. All rights reserved. Reprinted by permission of The Viking Press, Inc., and Mr. G. T. Sassoon.

"Babylon" by Siegfried Sassoon. From *Collected Poems* by Siegfried Sassoon. Copyright 1936, 1964 by Siegfried Sassoon. Reprinted by permission of The Viking Press, Inc., and Mr. G. T. Sassoon.

"The End of the World" by Archibald MacLeish. From *Collected Poems* 1917–1952 by Archibald MacLeish. Reprinted by permission of Houghton Mifflin Company.

"The Maid-Servant at the Inn" by Dorothy Parker. From *The Portable Dorothy Parker.* Copyright 1928, © 1956 by Dorothy Parker. Reprinted by permission of The Viking Press, Inc.

"At a Calvary Near the Ancre" and "The Parable of the Old Man and the Young" by Wilfred Owen. From Wilfred Owen, *Collected Poems.* Copyright Chatto & Windus, Ltd. 1946, © 1963. Reprinted by permission of New Directions Publishing Corporation, the Executors of the Estate of Harold Owen, and Chatto & Windus, Ltd.

"Divine Justice" by C. S. Lewis, from *The Pilgrim's Regress* by C. S. Lewis. Reprinted by permission of William B. Eerdmans Publishing Company and Collins Publishers.

"Simon the Cyrenian Speaks" by Countee Cullen, from *On These I Stand* by Countee Cullen. Copyright 1925 by Harper and Row, Publishers, Inc.; renewed 1953 by Ida M. Cullen.

"The Litany of the Dark People" by Countee Cullen, from *On These I Stand* by Countee Cullen. Copyright 1927 by Harper and Row, Publishers, Inc.; renewed 1955 by Ida M. Cullen. Reprinted by permission of Harper and Row, Publishers, Inc.

"Seven Stanzas at Easter" by John Updike. Copyright © 1961 by John Updike. Reprinted from *Telephone Poles and Other Poems* by John Updike, by permission of Alfred A. Knopf, Inc.

"The Nativity" and "Stephen to Lazarus" by C. S. Lewis. From *Poems of C. S. Lewis* edited by Walter Hooper, Copyright © 1964 by the Executors of the Estate of C. S. Lewis. Reprinted by permission of Harcourt Brace Jovanovich, Inc. and Curtis Brown, Ltd.

*To all of my wonderful students of
"The Bible as Literature" who, by their
enthusiasm, made this book possible.*

Foreword

One of the most popular courses we offer to the students of Julia Richman High School is Mrs. Vedral's Bible as Literature course. Term after term, students ask to have it given, and every term since its inception, we have offered at least one and more often two sections of this elective. One memorable term, five sections had to open.

The course originated out of our need to offer our students fresh material that would re-awaken their interest in the classroom. Traditional English was suffering in much the same way as traditional math, foreign language, and science were. Students were simply not coming to class. As a department, we decided to try to create courses that could be given in lieu of regular English courses for the same credit.

Mrs. Vedral was at first hesitant about starting a course in the Bible. Her background as a long-time student of the Bible eminently qualified her, and yet she was wary of possible dangers. She was then new to the secondary level, and her previous experience in the elementary school was of little help in work with inner-city adolescents. But with encouragement, her natural enthusiasm won out over her hesitation, and she began her planning.

The course as it stands today is not the course that was offered that first term. What is taught today has emerged from a constant re-working of the material used in that first session. It is always difficult to account for the sudden popularity of anything, but surely regular re-evaluation in terms of student needs and response is an important factor for success

in an academic setting. However, no one could deny that Joyce
Vedral's dynamic enthusiasm and her genuine knowledge of
the subject makes an unbeatable combination. What student
could ask for more?

ELEANOR K. FRIEDMAN
Assistant Principal (Supervision)
English
Board of Education of the City of New York
The Julia Richman High School
317 East 67th Street
New York, New York   10021

To the Teacher

Although this book contains material on the entire Bible, it is up to you to decide what is best suited to the needs of your students, and to formulate your own course outline. There is enough material here for two semesters; however, by being selective, you can have a one-semester course.

The key to my own success in teaching this course has been controversy. Rather than avoid controversial issues related to the Bible, I have made it a practice to delve into them head-first. The students enjoy giving their own views on such topics as miracles, the divinity of Christ, evolution, etc. Although we have never solved an issue yet, the time goes fast, and the class is rarely boring.

Another source of enjoyment for the students is the guest speakers. We invite a rabbi, a priest and a Protestant minister to come and speak on a given topic, such as "The Messiah." They speak on different days. The students are allowed to ask questions after each presentation. Then, in an essay, they are asked to compare the speakers' views on "The Messiah" and to give their own view. The students show amazing insight and growth in their essays.

The sections of "Special Studies" and "Poetry" may be used at your discretion when they are best suited to the needs of your class.

A word about the teacher's position as moderator is in order here. I have found that by withholding my own view on the many issues which come up in teaching such a course, I have had the freedom of anonymity. When asked what I believe, I simply state that my view isn't important, and I'd rather not state it at this time. In this way, most students feel free to express themselves without fear of censure.

To the Students

This book is not one of answers, but of questions, questions designed to make you think your way through the Bible. What happens after death? Who made the devil? Will the world end as stated in Matthew 24?

While you're doing all this deep thinking, you will also be reading the most well-read book in the world, and many of you will in the end, know more about the Bible than the average college English teacher.

After taking this course, you will also begin to notice quotations from the Bible in novels, plays, poems, historical documents, and even in popular songs.

You will be given a chance to express your own point of view on many issues, such as the Bible's position on sex, the existence of God, miracles, evolution, etc. No one has "The Answer." The aim of this course will not be to make anyone change his opinions, but rather to teach what is in the Bible.

Contents

Preface

The biblical interpretation of man has permeated various art forms in Western Civilization ever since the beginnings of the Judeo-Christian tradition. The one event, however, which insured that scriptural concepts would play a major role in the development of English and American literature was Constantine's decision by A.D. 313 to recognize Christianity as a legitimate religion within the Roman Empire. This decision eventually led to a state-supported church which totally dominated the social, political, and cultural life of Europe throughout the Middle Ages and during most of the early Renaissance. The total predominance of Christianity meant that practically all Europeans (and this includes the early inhabitants of Great Britain) thought almost exclusively in biblical terms. They interpreted life as they believed the Bible did, and thus its concepts are to be found in the art forms in which they expressed themselves. Because literature and the Bible are so similar in structure and function, it was only natural for these early writers, such as the authors of *Beowulf, Sir Gawain and the Green Knight,* and *The Canterbury Tales,* to build upon the biblical perspective, even as they perhaps modified it to some degree.

Even after the solidarity of the church was disrupted by Luther and Calvin on the Continent and by King Henry VIII in England, the biblical perspective maintained its influence upon the minds of men. When Shakespeare sat down to write *King Lear,* because of what literature is, and because he was so deeply influenced by scriptural concepts, he expressed his

vision of life in biblical terms. Lear commits the "sin" of pride
at the beginning of the play, learns to "lose his life in order to
gain it" during the course of the action, and achieves a kind
of "redemption" at the end, as he is "forgiven" by his daughter
Cordelia. John Milton, in *Paradise Lost, Paradise Regained,*
and *Samson Agonistes,* deals directly with specific biblical passages as he seeks to explain in new ways God's interpretation
of man. These examples could be expanded indefinitely. Close
study reveals that even those works of English literature
which make no direct mention of the Bible are steeped in its
terminology; they may not agree with the biblical interpretation of man, but they do make extensive use of that interpretation in whole or in part.

When Englishmen came to the New World, it was for a com-
plex set of reasons. Historians argue about those reasons, but
they would not deny that religious motives were among the
most significant. Early Americans were transplanted Englishmen working within basically the same religious framework as
Shakespeare and Milton. Although literature grew slowly in
the new American soil, from the very beginning it was
biblically oriented. Anne Bradstreet and Edward Taylor, two
of the earliest American writers, made extensive use of the
Bible in their attempt to apply God's word to the unique
American situation.

After 1700, the content of theological systems on both sides
of the Atlantic began to shift. Many people were moving
slowly away from "the faith of their fathers" and toward a
kind of belief which they thought was more in tune with
scientific and theological developments of the day. In some
ways, we may say that this movement has continued right
down to the present, and there are many scholars who feel that
the word which most aptly describes modern culture is "secular." Does this therefore mean that since 1700 literature has
made less and less use of the Bible and that today's novels and
poems and plays are devoid of scriptural content? It is true
that poetry like Taylor's or Milton's has all but vanished from
the scene, but it is certainly not true that indirect expressions

of biblical perspectives have disappeared in modern literature.

Nathaniel Hawthorne, perhaps the first truly great American novelist, did not wholly share the Christian commitment of his Puritan ancestors, but his vision of the human predicament is expressed in terms that come right out of the book of Romans. In story after story, Hawthorne points to the depraved human heart as the source of all evil and cruelty in man's experience. Herman Melville, even more militant than Hawthorne in his rejection of traditional Christianity, nevertheless relies heavily upon Scripture for names of characters (Ishmael and Ahab are the main characters in *Moby Dick*), for background explanation of his plots (a sermon about Jonah at the beginning of *Moby Dick* provides an incisive commentary on later action in the book), and for moral commentary on people and events (the hero's death in *Billy Budd* takes on immense significance because Melville likens it to the crucifixion). William Faulkner in the twentieth century has continued this trend by writing novels in which the action takes place on Easter weekend (*The Sound and the Fury*), in which biblical stories play a major evaluative role (*Absalom, Absalom*), and in which characters bear a distinct resemblance, either superficially or profoundly, to certain aspects of Christ's personality (Joe Christmas in *Light in August*). Hawthorne, Melville, and Faulkner are just three of the authors who write in this way, and the examples could be expanded almost endlessly.

This is not to say that all English and American literature is religious or Christian. Nothing could be further from the truth. The point is that biblical concepts, ideas, perspectives, names, and stories continue to be utilized with great frequency by secular writers. There is a vast amount of literature, both ancient and modern, both English and American, which simply cannot be properly understood without a basic knowledge of the Hebrew-Christian Scriptures. Literature and the Bible are both interpretations of human existence — they both perform the same function in men's lives. Because of this relationship, and because the Judeo-Christian heritage has played such a major role in the development of Western Civilization, literary artists, regardless of their own attitudes toward Judaism or Christianity, have adopted major elements of the biblical idiom in order to tell their stories. The purpose of this book is to make available in simplified form a brief summary and explanation of that idiom. Mastery of the idiom will make comprehension of the great works of world literature — from *The Divine Comedy* to *Couples,* from *Paradise Lost* to *Waiting for Godot* — a much more realizable goal.

SAMUEL T. LOGAN, JR., Chairman
Division of Literature and Language
Barrington College
Barrington, Rhode Island

A LITERARY SURVEY
OF THE BIBLE

Introduction

The Bible is an ancient book, and before we look at it directly, it will help us to know more about ancient books in general. The term "ancient" refers to the events of history prior to A.D. 476, the date of the final collapse of the Roman Empire in the West. Printing by means of movable type only came into common use in Europe in the fifteenth century, about a thousand years after the end of ancient history. Prior to that, all books had to be copied by hand, and even then, only a relative handful of people could read them.

How then did the content of ancient books become known to the bulk of ancient and medieval men? Many books have come down to us from ancient times and many of them are of great length, such as the epics of Homer. From what we can understand, these sagas, legends, and histories of ancient men were preserved among the people by oral tradition; in Greece, one could make a living as a troubadour, traveling about from place to place reciting and singing the great sagas and epics from memory. The Bible contains many allusions and references to the use of memorization and oral tradition, the most famous being in Deuteronomy:

And these words which I command you this day shall be upon your heart; and you shall teach them diligently to your children, and shall talk of them when you sit in your house, and when you walk by the way, and when you lie down, and when you rise. And you shall bind them as a sign upon your hand, and they shall be as frontlets between your eyes. And you shall write them on the doorposts of your house and on your gates.

(Deut. 6:6–9 RSV)

The capacity of ancient men to memorize was more highly developed, through necessity, than that of men today, and we must not judge the accuracy of oral tradition by our own faltering abilities in the area of memorization. Even Jesus, who himself never wrote a book, undoubtedly relied on the common practice among rabbis in his day of teaching his disciples to memorize his sayings. In any society where printing has not made books available to the mass of the people, the ability of that people to memorize has been highly developed.

However, writing was known and practiced in the ancient Near East well back into the patriarchal era (*ca.* 2000 B.C.). In fact, some of the earliest discoveries of writing have been made in the setting of the Bible, the Near East. Writing was originally done on stone, clay tablets, or leather. In its earliest forms, it consisted of stylized pictures that gradually became symbols from which letters evolved. Another peculiarity of ancient writing was the absence of vowels; words were written solely with consonants. Hebrew retains this peculiarity and is technically without vowels. One famous example of this is the name of God: transliterated into our system from Hebrew it reads YHWH. How does one pronounce such a conglomerate of letters? Fortunately, scholars have learned much about Hebrew vowel patterns, even in this century, so that we can be reasonably certain it was pronounced "Yahweh." In the English Bible, this word is most commonly translated as "Lord."

The Old Testament

It is very possible that some of the earliest events recorded in the Bible were reduced to writing around 2000 B.C. From that time on, the Old Testament began to take shape. The Bible did not drop from heaven as a single piece: it took over forty men and more than two thousand years before it took its present form. One of the largest parts of the Bible, consisting of Genesis, Exodus, Leviticus, Numbers, and Deuteronomy (called the Books of Moses), is the Torah or Pentateuch. It is an intriguing web of the history of a people with their God and the record of the law they say he gave them. The rest of the Old Testament is in two basic parts, "the writings" (historical-poetical books) and "the prophets." By 1000 B.C., some of these books, especially the Torah (law), were being brought together under one cover. This process continued gradually, so that what we know as the Old Testament had virtually come into being at least 250 years before Christ. By the end of the first century of the Christian era, the present collection of thirty-nine books was firmly fixed.

Through this same thousand-year period, certain practices began to be adopted for the transcription of the written text of the Old Testament books. Each scroll was copied carefully by hand. To insure accuracy, a standard computation of the number of letters in each line was kept; if a scribe discovered upon counting the letters of his own work that he had failed to come up with the correct number, he would be compelled to find his error and correct it or destroy his work and begin anew. Once an accurate copy had been made from an older certified copy, that older copy was then ceremonially destroyed. This practice left us, until recently, with no truly ancient copies of the Old Testament in Hebrew, the oldest dating back no earlier than A.D. 900.

Then in 1947 came a major breakthrough: scrolls and fragments dating back to 300 B.C. were discovered in some long-forgotten caves overlooking the Dead Sea. Here at last were portions of the Old Testament copied 1000 years earlier than any manuscript known to exist before 1947. Scholars found fragments and some lengthy portions of almost every one of the thirty-nine books. This would be the first objective test of the accuracy of the copying system used for the sacred writings, and scholars were able to report better-than-expected results from their comparisons. No significant changes in the text could be detected, the only differences being in matters like the spelling of a word or the choice of a synonym.

THE NEW TESTAMENT

In comparison with the Old Testament, the New Testament
came into being almost overnight. Only about fifty years were
required for its compilation. The New Testament is commonly
broken into four parts: the Gospels, the Acts, the Letters, and
the Revelation (Apocalypse). As the story of Jesus was spread
through the Mediterranean world by missionaries, congregations of Christian believers began to spring up in various cities
and localities. The missionaries (apostles) and church leaders
would have occasion to write letters to these congregations
about various matters. So, throughout the period A.D. 40–90,
these letters that were to become part of the New Testament
were being written. During the same years, the sayings and
acts of Jesus began to be written down. These documents have
come to be called "Gospels" (good news). They are not biography in the strict sense because of the enormous emphasis placed
upon the death and resurrection of Jesus, which was the core of
the good news the early Christians proclaimed. Mark's Gospel
is likely the earliest, followed by Matthew and Luke, who is also
responsible for the Book of Acts, the history of the early church
with special attention to the life of the apostle Paul. The
Fourth Gospel (John) was probably written between A.D. 80
and 90. Sometime in the last decade of the first century, John
was exiled to the isle of Patmos off Asia Minor. There he reports to have received revelations and visions concerning
heaven and the end of the world. His book is called the Revelation of St. John the Divine ("divine" does not mean heavenly,
but that he was a theologian). (See p. 149.)

During the second and third centuries, these twenty-seven
"books" (some of them no more than a page long) became accepted as Scripture, equal in status to the Old Testament books
among the churches. Final official ratification of these books by
the western church was made by the Council of Carthage (A.D.
397).

The New Testament is the most heavily attested ancient
book known to man. That means that it has more and older

manuscripts than any other book coming down to us from ancient days. Unlike that of the Old Testament, the copying process for the New Testament did not provide for the systematic destruction of the older manuscripts, and so we have discovered a fragment of the Gospel of John that dates back to the end of the first century, placing it within thirty years of the original writing of that document. Before the discovery of that fragment in the twentieth century, such a thing was believed impossible for any ancient book.

It is interesting to compare the manuscript support for the *History of the Peloponnesian War* by the famous Greek historian Thucydides, written between 423 and 403 B.C. The earliest extant manuscript of this book dates back only to A.D. 900, 1300 years after its original writing by Thucydides. Similarly, the earliest manuscripts of Plato are dated at least a thousand years after the death of that great philosopher and student of Socrates.

The Bible and the English Language

Even in ancient times, the Bible was translated into other languages. The Old Testament was translated into Greek in Alexandria, Egypt, about two centuries before Christ. During this same period, Syriac and Latin editions began to appear. After the beginning of the Christian era, the church became largely responsible for translating the Scriptures of both the Old and New Testaments into the tongues of those lands where its message had taken root.

Christianity began to take root in the British Isles probably earlier than A.D. 200, but for a long time we know of no Bible translations. Various tribes inhabited those islands, with sometimes widely varying languages, so the missionaries probably translated orally on-the-spot. In the next few centuries, Anglo-Saxon became the dominant language, and though no Bible was produced in that language, biblical stories were translated into songs and poetry in the seventh century by Caedmon. In the eighth century, more work was done by various church scholars, so that various Psalms, the Ten Commandments, and the Gospel of John were extant in Anglo-Saxon (Old English). This process was continued into the Middle Ages. In 1066, the Normans conquered England, wresting it from the Anglo-Saxons, and introduced the French language to the isles. The combination of Anglo-Saxon and French began to produce what we now refer to as "Middle English," the language of Chaucer.

It was in the era of Middle English that the first complete Bible appeared in Britain in the vernacular. This was the work of John Wycliffe, who did his work with the average man in mind. Previous translations had been made primarily for the use of the clergy, but Wycliffe wanted to put the Scriptures in the hands of laymen. This was in the late fourteenth century, and Wycliffe was intent upon a reformation of the whole church. Thus he organized the "poor priests," or Lollards, who traveled throughout Britain preaching to and teaching the common people. His Bible enjoyed wide usage among all levels of society for over one hundred years.

In 1484, exactly one hundred years after the death of Wycliffe, William Tyndale was born. Much had happened in that intervening century. The English language had undergone a "vowel shift," producing basically the same language we speak today, Modern English. This alone made a new translation imperative, but a number of other factors determined the nature of that translation. Between 1450 and 1500, printing with movable type came into wide use in Europe. At the same time, the spread of the Ottoman Empire had driven the Christian Greek and Hebrew scholars of Constantinople into Western Europe. These and other events made the sixteenth century a time of great intellectual stimulation, and it was in this time that William Tyndale translated the Bible.

Wycliffe had translated from the Latin, but now Tyndale could translate from the original Greek and Hebrew. Wycliffe had to publish by means of hand-copying; Tyndale had the printing press at his disposal. Tyndale received greater immediate opposition than did Wycliffe, so much that he published his first edition of the New Testament in Germany under the protection of the Lutherans and had to smuggle it into England. But it became the model for all other translations into the twentieth century, and it was virtually the catalyst that formed English as a literary language. The importance of Tyndale's work can hardly be overstated.

Before we go on to briefly examine the various English translations since Tyndale, we should mention some of the specific opposition he and Wycliffe received. In Wycliffe's time, state and church authorities forbade Bible reading in the vernacular on pain of death. Later, the Lollard movement had become so popular that Wycliffe's body was exhumed and burned. Ever since 1415, his Bible had been condemned and consigned to the flames. Tyndale had to flee to the Continent, and there he finally experienced martyrdom, being strangled and burned in Antwerp on October 6, 1536. Through the Middle Ages, the church had begun to reason that only trained clergy should read and interpret the Scriptures, that the average man would be unable to formulate correct interpretation if left to himself. Today, almost no branch of the church holds strictly to this view, but we see something of the turmoil of those centuries of transition by the vehemence with which the view was held then and what it cost men like Tyndale.

Several versions appeared in the sixteenth century subsequent to Tyndale. Each of them has an interesting and peculiar story, but we do not have room to tell them here. Until this century, the new versions were all, basically, revisions of Tyndale's work, so we will list them with brief notes in chronological order.

The Coverdale Version (1535). The work of Miles Coverdale, an acquaintance of Tyndale, who claimed in his 1537 edition to have been granted a license from King Henry VIII to print the Bible.

The Thomas Matthew Bible (1537). A revision of Tyndale by

his friend John Rogers, a zealous Protestant, later burned at
the stake. ("Thomas Matthew" was Rogers' pseudonym.)

The Great Bible (1539). A revision of the Matthew Bible by
Miles Coverdale that was placed in the churches to be read by
the parishioners, hence its large size making it suitable for
public reading.

The Taverner Bible (1539). Done by a layman, Richard
Taverner, a Greek scholar from Oxford. Another revision of
Tyndale, it was the first English Bible to be printed in England
rather than on the continent.

The Geneva Bible (1560). With the accession of Mary Tudor to
the English throne, many Protestant scholars fled to Geneva,
the headquarters of John Calvin. Miles Coverdale was there
and headed up this revision of the Great Bible. It was smaller
and cheaper than its predecessors, and was also the first edition of the English Bible to have chapter and verse divisions.
It became very popular and went through 140 editions before
being displaced by the King James version.

The Bishop's Bible (1568). Because the Geneva Bible had become the Bible of the people and was a genuinely better translation than the Great Bible, Archbishop Parker called together
a group of scholars, many of them bishops, to revise the work.
It never entirely displaced the Great Bible, but it did provide
a solid basis for the King James version.

The Douay (Douai) Version (1609–10). The Roman church had
persistently relied upon the Latin Vulgate of Jerome (late
fourth century), the "common" Bible of the whole church from
early times through the Middle Ages. Now the proliferation of
Bibles in the vernacular tongues by European Protestants
made a Roman-English version imperative. The task was
undertaken in France at the English College in Douay, where
the Old Testament was done, and in Rheims, where the New

Testament was completed. It was a translation of the Latin, unlike the Protestant Bibles which had all gone back to Hebrew and Greek; however, scholars believe the Douay translators were strongly influenced by the Geneva Bible.

The King James Version (KJV) (1611). In 1604, James VI of Scotland became James I of England. That same year he ordered a new translation of the Bible, making this version the first to be so initiated. The work was undertaken by forty-six scholars, who broke down into committees, each responsible for certain sections of Scripture. As a given committee finished its work, the translation was sent to the other committees for their scrutiny and comment, so that the whole work was under constant review. This was unique procedure (even the Bishop's Bible translators did not do this), and it helped to produce the version that was to hold sway for over 300 years. The translators said in their preface, "We never thought from the beginning that we should need to make a new translation, nor yet to make a bad one a good one—but to make a good one better, or out of many good ones, one principal good one. . . ." History amply demonstrates that they succeeded. By the end of the seventeenth century, it had displaced all its predecessors as the Bible of the churches and of the common folk; even today, in the latter third of the twentieth century, it still holds its own as the most familiar of all English Bibles.

The English Revised Version (ERV) (1881–85). In 1867, Constantin von Tischendorf discovered an ancient Bible manuscript in a monastery atop Mount Sinai in the Sinai peninsula. This manuscript, called *Codex Sinaiticus,* contained the Old and New Testaments in Greek and was dated at around A.D. 300, making it about 700 years older than any manuscript that had been available to the translators of the Authorized Version (KJV). This discovery and others like it, together with shifts in English usage since the seventeenth century, made a revision highly desirable. The Church of England began the work, but invited representatives from every branch of Western Christendom to participate. Two committees of twenty-seven members each began their respective work on the Old and New Testaments in 1870. The New Testament was published in 1881, followed by the Old in 1885. Its public reception was spectacular: Oxford University Press received orders for one million copies before publication.

The American Standard Version (ASV) (1901). The American committee that participated in the revision of 1881–85 (ERV) had differed on some points with their British associates. Notably, they preferred to translate the Hebrew divine name, YHWH, as "Jehovah"—the British preferred "Lord." These differences were printed in an appendix of the ERV for fourteen years while the Americans agreed not to publish a separate edition. At the end of that period, the Americans issued the American Standard Version, embodying their preferences. They replaced the peculiarly British terms, and antiquated words, making it a more "modern" sounding translation to American ears.

The Modern Language Bible (1945–59). Commonly known as the Berkeley Version because Gerrit Verkuyl, the editor-in-chief of the project, resided in Berkeley, California. It is not a revision, but a new translation done by scholars of largely orthodox Protestant backgrounds. Some interpretative notes are included to aid the reader in his understanding of the text.

The Revised Standard Version (RSV) (1946–52). In 1929, the International Council of Religious Education purchased the copyright on the ASV and set about to revise it. Since 1901, many discoveries had been made in Greek and Hebrew syntax and idiom, making both languages much plainer to the modern translator. Because of the Great Depression, work was delayed until 1937. The work was done by committee review similar to the procedures used with KJV, ERV, and ASV. Their work maintained much of the beauty and flow of the KJV but was not restricted to pure revision—the translators were at liberty to make changes as they saw fit. Their work has stood the test of a quarter-century and has demonstrated a popularity that reflects its clarity, readability, and dignity.

The New English Bible (NEB) (1961–70). In 1946, George S. Hendry, a minister of the Church of Scotland, proposed to his church authorities that a translation of the Bible be made in the language of the present day. Virtually every Protestant group in the British Isles was represented on the joint committee that began its work in the Jerusalem Chamber, Westminster Abbey, January, 1948. Their New Testament appeared in 1961, followed nine years later by the Old Testament. The NEB is a wholly new translation, made without conscious reference to the KJV. It has been lauded for its readability, criticized for its "Britishisms."

The Jerusalem Bible (1966). This version is unique among English Bibles. In 1956, the Dominican Bible School in Jerusalem, a Roman Catholic institution, produced a translation in modern French that came to be known popularly as *La Bible de Jérusalem*. The Bible includes an extensive set of cross-references, introductory articles and annotations. In the English edition, done largely by British scholars and churchmen, these notes and introductions are taken directly from the French. The text of the Bible itself was done from the Hebrew and Greek, but with conscious reference to the work of the French scholars. In the Old Testament, the Hebrew divine name (YHWH) is rendered generally as "Yahweh."

The New American Bible (NAB) (1970). To quote from the introduction by Pope Paul VI, "For more than a quarter of a century, members of the Catholic Biblical Association of America, sponsored by the Bishops' Committee of the Confraternity of Christian Doctrine, have labored to create this new translation of the Scriptures from the original languages or from the oldest extant form in which they exist." This Catholic version, like the Jerusalem Bible, translates from the Greek and Hebrew, breaking from the Douay precedent of translation from the Latin. Unlike any former translation of the Roman church, this was executed entirely in the United States.

The New American Standard Version (NAS) (1960–71). This is a revision of the American Standard Version (ASV) of 1901. A group called the Lockman Foundation lamented the passing from the scene of the ASV which they cite as "a monumental product of applied scholarship, assiduous labor and thorough procedure." So they took it upon themselves to revise and update it for modern readers. The foundation lists its fourfold aim in its introduction to the Bible: "(1) These publications shall be true to the original Hebrew and Greek; (2) They shall be grammatically correct; (3) They shall be understandable to the masses; (4) They shall give the Lord Jesus Christ His proper place, the place which the Word gives Him; no work will ever be personalized."

Today's English Version (TEV) (1966). Although this version is not yet complete (the Old Testament has yet to be published in full), it deserves mention here because of its widespread circulation. The American Bible Society commissioned a fresh translation of the New Testament, which was published in an extremely inexpensive edition in 1966. One of its most notable features is the use of charming line-drawings to illustrate the text. This edition is entitled *Good News for Modern Man* (subtitle: *Today's English Version*) and has been more widely circulated among English-speaking peoples than any other book ever printed. It first sold for approximately twenty-five cents.

In the last three centuries, there have been many other translations and paraphrases of the Bible in English. Most of these have been the work of individual scholars, and each has enjoyed a degree of popularity. The versions listed above have been separately noted because they are the works, after Tyndale, of groups of men, and represent important milestones in the story of the English Bible.

A WORD ABOUT THE "CANON"

The word "canon" is derived from the same Greek word as the more familiar "cane." The stem meant basically "straight rod," and from that, "measuring rod." From there the meaning broadened to mean "rule" or "standard." Most philologists think that the Greek word was derived from an even more ancient Semitic stem meaning "rod" in Assyrian, Ugaritic, Hebrew, etc. How did such a word come to be associated with the Bible?

Since there were many religious books written in ancient times, a decision had to be made as to which were actually divinely inspired and therefore qualified to be set up as the rule or standard for the faith and life of the believers. So the word "canon" began to be used with regard to those books that were recognized in the community of belief to be from God. Today the word "canon," when used with reference to the Bible, simply means the list of the names of the books that are contained in the Bible. The tradition of over eighteen centuries has made most questions about the canonicity of various books seem quite out of place. It is inconceivable that any of the books now in the Bible could somehow be removed without the Bible in some measure ceasing any longer to be the Bible.

The stories and theories as to how the present books came to be regarded as canonical are conflicting and frequently unclear. Each theory inevitably represents the theorist's own opinion as to the divine source of the Scriptures. There is not room in this book to examine the various theories of canonization, but for the reader who is interested in pursuing this topic, the bibliography includes some books that deal with it (see pp. 169–72).

THE APOCRYPHA

Before we dismiss the matter of the canon, one item of signal importance remains. This is the question of the Apocrypha.

There are fourteen or fifteen books, not usually printed in Protestant and Jewish editions of the Old Testament, which do appear in Roman Catholic editions. Why is this?

None of these books appear in the Hebrew canon of the Old Testament, but with the exception of II Esdras, they all appear in the Greek version of the Old Testament known as the Septuagint. Their titles, as rendered by the Revised Standard Version, follow:

1   The First Book of Esdras
2   The Second Book of Esdras
3   Tobit
4   Judith
5   The Additions to the Book of Esther
6   The Wisdom of Solomon
7   Ecclesiasticus, or the Wisdom of Jesus the Son of Sirach
8   Baruch
9   The Letter of Jeremiah
10 The Prayer of Azariah and the Song of the Three Young Men
11 Susanna
12 Bel and the Dragon
13 The Prayer of Manasseh
14 The First Book of Maccabees
15 The Second Book of Maccabees

Most English editions of the Apocrypha include the Letter of Jeremiah in the book of Baruch, reducing the list to fourteen titles.

The Second Book of Esdras made its appearance in ancient times in the Old Latin translations of the Old Testament done from the Greek Septuagint. In the fourth century of the Christian era, Pope Damasus I commissioned the greatest biblical scholar of his day, Jerome, to translate the entire Bible afresh into Latin. His work produced the standard Latin text, known as the Vulgate, which ultimately displaced the Old Latin versions.

Jerome secured the services of rabbis who taught him Hebrew and counseled him in his rendering of the Old Testament. By translating from the Hebrew texts, Jerome was immediately faced with the problem of the Apocryphal books. Although they did not occur in his Hebrew manuscripts, he decided to take them from the Greek and include them in his Latin version. He prefaced each of the Apocryphal books with a note to the reader explaining their special situation. These prefaces were generally lost in subsequent editions, so that by medieval times, the church made almost no distinction between the Apocrypha and the rest of the Old Testament. In 1546, these books, with the exception of I and II Esdras and the Prayer of Manasseh, were formally canonized by the Roman Catholic church at the Council of Trent. After that, these books appeared scattered among the other Old Testament books, so that Tobit and Judith follow Nehemiah; the Wisdom of Solomon and Ecclesiasticus follow the Song of Solomon; Baruch (including the Letter of Jeremiah) follows Lamentations; I and II Maccabees stand at the end of the Old Testament.

The Protestants have not so recognized these books, and one generally finds them bound between the Testaments or as an appendix following the New Testament in Protestant editions of the Bible. Today most Protestant editions are issued with the Apocrypha totally absent. This, of course, has always been true of Jewish editions.

One may ask, what is the nature of these books and where did they come from originally? Emerging out of the intertestamental period, roughly 350 B.C.–A.D. 40, they are a combination of historical books, moralistic novellas, wisdom literature, psalms, devotional and liturgical work, and one apocalypse, II Esdras. The inter-testamental period was a time when Greek culture entered Israel through the military conquests of Alexander the Great. The terrific upheaval of Jewish life is reflected in the books of the Apocrypha.

Consult the bibliography for further reading (pp. 169–72).

THE ARRANGEMENT OF THE BOOKS OF THE BIBLE

The Hebrew Old Testament is arranged under three categories: the Law (Torah), the Prophets (Nebhi-im), and the Writings (Kethubhim):

THE LAW

1 Genesis
2 Exodus
3 Leviticus
4 Numbers
5 Deuteronomy

THE PROPHETS

Former
1 Joshua
2 Judges
3 Samuel
4 Kings

Latter
5 Isaiah
6 Jeremiah
7 Ezekiel
8 The Twelve (Hosea–Malachi)

THE WRITINGS

Poetical
1 Psalms
2 Proverbs
3 Job

Rolls
4 Song of Solomon
5 Ruth
6 Lamentations
7 Ecclesiastes
8 Esther

Books
9 Daniel
10 Ezra–Nehemiah
11 Chronicles

The Greek Old Testament (Septuagint) contains the books in a different order. This is the order familiar to modern readers around the world.

LAW	HISTORY	
Genesis	Joshua	I and II Chronicles
Exodus	Judges	Ezra
Leviticus	Ruth	Nehemiah
Numbers	I & II Samuel	Esther
Deuteronomy	I & II Kings	

POETRY	MAJOR PROPHETS
Job	Isaiah
Psalms	Jeremiah
Proverbs	Lamentations
Ecclesiastes	Ezekiel
Song of Solomon	Daniel

MINOR PROPHETS		
Hosea	Jonah	Zephaniah
Joel	Micah	Haggai
Amos	Nahum	Zechariah
Obadiah	Habakkuk	Malachi

The books of the New Testament have been arranged in various orders during the history of the church. One early order for the four Gospels was Matthew, John, Mark, and Luke, placing the books done by the original apostles who had accompanied Jesus first. However, the following arrangement is by far the most common:

GOSPELS	HISTORY
Matthew	Acts
Mark	
Luke	
John	

Paul's letters (arranged in order of length, longest first, shortest last)

Romans	Colossians
I & II Corinthians	I & II Thessalonians
Galatians	I & II Timothy
Ephesians	Titus
Philippians	Philemon

The Letter to the Hebrews (the author does not give his name, and several theories have been propounded about its authorship).

The Catholic (General) Letters

James	I, II, & III John
I & II Peter	Jude

The Apocalypse or Book of Revelation

SUMMARY OF BIBLICAL CONTENT

Genesis	The beginnings. Adam and Eve to Joseph's death.
Exodus	The enslavement and escape of the Hebrews. The ten commandments and the rest of the law.
Leviticus	A detailed description of the law and sacrifice.
Numbers	The forty years of wandering in the wilderness.
Deuteronomy	A repetition of the law.
Joshua	The conquest of Canaan, the promised land.
Judges	The period of judges in Israel.
Ruth	The short story of a faithful servant of God.
I & II Samuel	The prophet Samuel, kings Saul and David.

I & II Kings	Kings David, Solomon, prophets Elijah and Elisha, and the divided Kingdom.
I & II Chronicles	Repeats much of I and II Kings.
Ezra	A record of the return of the Jews from captivity.
Nehemiah	The rebuilding of the walls of Jerusalem.
Esther	How Queen Esther saves the Jews from death.
Job	The testing of a good man.
Psalms	Songs and poems of praise.
Proverbs	Wise sayings about how to live.
Ecclesiastes	On the vanity of life "under the sun."
Song of Solomon	A love poem.
Isaiah	The prophet of promise and woe.
Jeremiah	The "weeping prophet." Backsliding and restoration.
Lamentations	Jeremiah laments the affliction of Israel.
Ezekiel	Decries the sad condition of Israel, speaks of a better day coming.
Daniel	A faithful servant of God during the captivity. Interprets dreams and prophecies of the last days.
Hosea	Lived during the time of Isaiah. Rebukes Israel for sin.
Joel	Speaks of national repentance and coming blessing.
Amos	Five visions. Denounces injustice, oppression of the poor, and selfishness.
Obadiah	Speaks of the doom of Edom and the deliverance of Israel.
Jonah	The reluctant missionary and his stay in a fish.
Micah	Tells of the depravity of Israel, calls for repentance.

Nahum	Prophesies the destruction of Nineveh and the deliverance of Judah from Assyria.
Habakkuk	Speaks of God's great care.
Zephaniah	Threatens Israel for sinning and tells of the future glory.
Haggai	Warns the people to build a second temple.
Zechariah	Also warns the people to build the temple. He has eight visions.
Malachi	Final messages to a rebellious people.
Matthew	Tells of the life, teachings, and death of Jesus Christ. Emphasizes the "messianic" quality of Christ.
Mark	Tells of the life and teachings of Christ, but emphasizes the supernatural power of Christ. This is the first Gospel written.
Luke	Also tells of the life and teachings of Christ, but emphasizes the physical quality of Christ's ministry. (Luke was a physician.) Luke contains the most complete biography of Christ.
John	Also tells of the life and teachings of Christ, but emphasizes the divinity of Christ.
Acts	Tells how Christianity was spread by the followers of Christ.
Romans	A letter to Christians at Rome from Paul in which he states his doctrine in its most complete form.
I & II Corinthians	Letters to the church at Corinth in which the author rebukes various sins and re-asserts the doctrines of Christianity.
Galatians	A letter to the Galatian church in which justification by faith and not works is emphasized.

Ephesians	A letter to Ephesus in which the plan of salvation is discussed.
Philippians	A letter to Philippi in which Paul teaches about fellowship and self-emptying.
Colossians	A letter to the Colossian church telling of the glory of Christ.
I & II Thessalonians	Discusses the future return of Christ.
I & II Timothy	A young pastor is counseled in matters of church-life.
Titus	Another letter to a pastor.
Philemon	Paul's appeal on behalf of a runaway slave, now converted.
Hebrews	Links the Old and New Testaments through a discussion of sacrifice.
James	Faith and works.
I & II Peter	Encouragement in the face of trouble and persecution.
I, II, & III John	God's forgiveness, brotherly love, and worldliness.
Jude	Warnings against sin and immorality are given.
Revelation	The end of time is revealed. The battle between good and evil, in which good triumphs, is dramatized.

The Chronology of Biblical Times

When dealing with events which occurred some five thousand years ago, it is dangerous to be too dogmatic about dates, even if one is an accomplished scholar. The reasons for this are obvious. We simply do not have enough "primary sources" to which we can refer. For this reason, you will find that there is some degree of latitude even within an individual scholar's estimate of the dating of biblical events. And, of course, different scholars vary greatly in their estimates. The following dates are approximate, but well within the range of most scholars' opinions. The dates of Abraham and the Exodus are the most disputed. (Refer to the bibliography for further information.)

B.C.

2200	Abraham leaves Ur of the Chaldees to follow God's call.
1350	The "Exodus" from Egypt, followed by forty years of wandering in the "wilderness."
1050–1017	Saul's reign in Israel.
1017–977	David's reign in Israel.
977–937	Solomon's reign in Israel.
974	The first Temple begun in the fourth year of Solomon's reign.
937	Upon Solomon's death, the kingdom is divided into two kingdoms, the northern one Israel and the southern one Judah (I Kings 12).
722	The fall of Samaria (capital of Israel) to the Assyrians. The end of the kingdom of Israel. (The ten northern tribes are never reunited again.)
701	Jerusalem is besieged by the Assyrians, but not captured.
606	The Babylonians take both Jerusalem and the Assyrian capital of Nineveh. Ten thousand leading Jews are carried off to Babylon.
586	The destruction of Jerusalem. Captivity begins.
536	Cyrus, king of Persia, having conquered Babylonia, permits many Jews to return to Jerusalem.
516	Completion of the second Temple.
458	Further return of Jews from Babylon under Ezra.
334	Alexander the Great invades Persia.
330	End of the Persian Empire.
323	Death of Alexander. In the succeeding period,

	Palestine becomes subject to Egypt again, and then to Syria.
167	Persecution by Antiochus Epiphanes, king of Syria, and his desecration of the Temple lead to a successful Jewish revolt, under the Maccabee family. (The account of this is contained in the Apocrypha.)
165	Rededication of the Temple.
63	Pompey, the Roman general, conquers Judea, ending Jewish independence until our own time. The Herods became Roman appointees.
37–4	Reign of Herod the Great. Since Jesus was born during his reign, incurring his jealousy (see Gospel accounts), we must date the birth of Jesus as taking place near 5 B.C.
5	The birth of Christ.

A.D.

30	The crucifixion of Jesus at Jerusalem.
36	The conversion of Saul of Tarsus (Paul) on the road to Damascus.
50	Council at Jerusalem agrees to accept uncircumcised persons as members of the Christian church.
66	The martyrdom of Paul at Rome. The Jews go to war with the Romans.
70	The fall of Jerusalem. The destruction of the Temple. (The Temple has never been rebuilt, even to this day. It is the hope of many devout Jews to see this Temple rebuilt.) The dispersion of the Jews. (In 1947, the Jewish people acquired the territory of Palestine, and once again began to come together as a nation. Many devout Jews see this as a fulfillment of Old Testament prophecy, and as the last step before the rebuilding of the Temple.)

The Old Testament

The Pentateuch

In the German Bible, Genesis is simply titled *The First Book of Moses,* while Exodus, Leviticus, Numbers, and Deuteronomy are referred to respectively as the second, third, fourth, and fifth books of Moses. Moses is the traditional author of these books, and the central human character of all but Genesis.

His authorship has been challenged, especially in the last two centuries, by scholars engaged in "source critical" and "form critical" studies. They insist that the Torah (the five books of Moses) could not possibly have been the work of Moses and, instead, generally attribute the work to about five different authors or sources. The technical nature of their arguments precludes a lengthy treatment of them here, and the reader is referred to the bibliography. While one will soon discover that this matter of authorship is hotly disputed among scholars, it is hardly mentioned in the books under consideration. In several cases, Moses is instructed to write down the words he hears from God (*e.g.,* Exod. 34:27). In later biblical documents, the Pentateuch (from the Greek, meaning "five books") is referred to as "the law of Moses" (Dan. 9:11), "the book of Moses" (II Chron. 35:12), and when quotes are taken from one of these books, they are frequently prefaced by "Moses said" (Mark 7:10).

The titles of the individual books (Genesis, Exodus, Leviticus, Numbers, Deuteronomy) came from Greek and Latin sources attached around the time that the Septuagint was compiled. In the original Hebrew, they had represented one continuous piece, but their length made it impossible to in-

clude them all on a single scroll. So today, the book divisions
are based on the amount of writing that could conveniently be
contained on a single scroll. As it happened, the Torah required
five separate scrolls.

GENESIS

When, some years ago, a movie was produced entitled *The
Bible,* it was based entirely on the narrative of Genesis. Such
is the importance of this first book of the Bible. It sets the stage
for all of the remaining sixty-five books of the canon, and without a basic grasp of its contents, no reader can fully understand
the others.

The Greek word *genesis* means "origin," "beginning," or
"source." The book describes man's moral, physical, and
spiritual decline from the Garden of Eden to a coffin in Egypt.
The first eleven chapters form a special unit of primeval history, covering the creation and fall of man, Cain's murder of
his brother, the flood, and the episode of the tower of Babel.
Each of these stories represents an instance of man's rebellion
met by God's judgment and mercy, in that order. After the con-
fusion of tongues at Babel, God's mercy is expressed in the call
of Abraham, who was promised that his progeny would be as
the sand of the sea. The book then focuses on the emerging
covenant people of God, with absorbing tales of the great
patriarchs of Israel: Abraham, Isaac, and Jacob. Genesis concludes with one of the finest examples of the short story to
come down to us from ancient times, the Joseph story.

CREATION
THE FALL OF MAN
(Gen. 1–3)

1. What did God create on each of the seven days?
2. In Genesis 1:28, God tells Adam and Eve to "be fruitful

and multiply, and replenish the earth." Can this be used
to argue a case against birth control? What if Adam and
Eve had practiced birth control?

3. Why did God forbid Adam and Eve to eat from the tree
   of the knowledge of good and evil?
4. In what sense did Adam and Eve "die" when they ate of
   the tree?
5. What is the original sin, according to Genesis 3?
6. How do we know that Adam and Eve realized they had
   done wrong?
7. Compare the creation story of the Bible with the creation
   story of Babylonia. (See notes below for a Babylonian account.)
8. What are the judgments on Adam, Eve, and the serpent?
   Can you prove or disprove the historicity of the biblical
   account?

Evolution and the Bible: One of the largest areas of dispute
in biblical studies centers around the creation of the world.
In the eighteenth and nineteenth centuries, philosophical as-
sumptions began to shift; evolutionary theories about the
origin of our planet and universe began to be much more popular than catastrophic theories. This popularity has continued
into our century, so that today, evolutionism has become a
veritable touchstone of faith in departments of anthropology
and biology of universities in the western world.

Very much in response to this trend, three major positions
have grown up among Bible students as to how one ought to
regard the record of Genesis 1–3. We will label these three
positions the literal, the figurative, and the mythical interpretations.

Proponents of the literal interpretation argue that the
world was created in six twenty-four-hour days by God calling
into full-blown existence things that theretofore did not exist.
They point to geological evidences used by the catastrophists,
asserting that the flood of Genesis 7–8 was indeed the universal
catastrophe that explains it all. Theories of evolution, literal-

ists point out, violate the second law of thermodynamics, which states that things invariably tend to disintegrate, i.e., to move from a state of order to one of disorder. They are always quick to note that evolution is a theory, not an established fact, and that science has produced much data that does not support evolutionary theory.

The figurative interpretation is favored by those who want to believe in the Bible and to accept evolution. They are convinced that both are correct, and that there is no contradiction between them. The sequence of creation in Genesis 1, they observe, corresponds roughly to certain sequences of evolution, e.g., the first animate life occurs in the sea. They do not believe the "days" of Genesis 1 to be twenty-four-hour periods, but regard them as figurative indications of great geologic eras. The Bible, they say, does not explain *how* the earth and all its foliage and creatures came to be, it only explains *why* they came to be. In this way, science is given one area of responsibility (mechanics and procedural theory) while religion is assigned another role (philosophy and elevated theory). The figurativists hope that this division will keep peace, so that scientists can go to church on Sunday, and religionists can go to school on Monday, and not fight.

The third position, we have called "the mythical." This stance is adopted by those who are convinced that science (the theory of evolution) is right and that the Bible is therefore patently incorrect, especially in Genesis 1–3. They say that God has chosen to communicate to us by means of myths, legends, fables, and folk stories. These stories are not true (i.e., not historically accurate), but they tell the truth, and so the mythicists accept them for purely religious purposes. (Apart from these purposes, of course, the documents are virtually worthless.)

In all fairness, we should note in conclusion that there are men of considerable knowledge in every area of academic endeavor who fit in each of our three categories. There are learned anthropologists and geologists, for instance, who are literalists; the same is true for the figurativists and the mythicists. This does not mean they are all right. If any one position is ever conclusively proven, the other two will be simultaneously disproven.

Other Creation Stories: The Babylonian account of the creation of the universe differs greatly from that of the Bible. In the Babylonian account, the world is created by a struggle in the forces of nature. Man is created as a slave to the gods. Apsu, the god of fresh water, and Tiamat, the goddess of salt water, existed and had children. Ea, the earth and water god, organized the other gods and killed Apsu. Then the main god of Babylonia, Marduk, allied himself with the young gods and killed Tiamat. Marduk carved Tiamat's body in half. From one half he made the sky, from the other half the earth. From the bones of a murdered god, he created man, a savage killer.

Original Sin: The doctrine of original sin is accepted by Christians. They see the "fall" as recorded in Genesis, when Adam and Eve disobeyed God and ate from the forbidden tree. Interestingly, the Christmas tree owes its origin to the tree in the Garden of Eden. During the early Middle Ages, mystery plays were popular in Europe. The tree in the Garden of Eden, called the paradise tree, was a stage prop in the re-enactment of the story of the "fall." It became customary to have a tree in the home around Christmas time as a reminder that man has fallen from the grace of God by a tree (original sin) and because of that Christ came into the world (Christmas) to purchase man's forgiveness by dying on a tree. (The cross is often called a tree.)

Birth Control: The Bible has been used to argue for and against birth control. Some argue that since God commanded Adam and Eve to replenish the earth, it is disobedient not to have children, strengthening their argument by citing the case in Genesis 38 when Onan spilled his semen on the ground, disobeying the law which required him to raise up a son for his dead brother. His disobedience, according to verse 10, displeased the Lord, so he slew Onan. People who favor birth control often refer to Christ's remarks in Matthew 24, warning about the woe to those who bear children in the last days.

CAIN COMMITS MURDER (Gen. 4:1–16)
THE FLOOD (Gen. 6–9)

1. Why did God accept Abel's offering and not Cain's?
2. How do you know that Cain really did not know God's power?
3. What was Cain's punishment?
4. Why did God want to destroy mankind?
5. Why was Noah picked to build the ark?
6. Why did Noah build an altar?
7. What covenant did God make with Noah?
8. Analyze Noah's curse upon Canaan. What does it mean?
9. How does the flood story in the Bible compare with the flood story told in *The Epic of Gilgamesh?*

The Mark of Cain: Most scholars believe that the mark upon Cain was in fact a tattoo. Some people have tried to show that the curse was being made "black," and have used this argument to justify the enslavement of the black man. The descendants of Cain were not black, and they were rulers, not slaves. They were, in fact, called the "Kenites" and were known to be a tattooed people. The important thing to note about Cain's mark was that it was meant to protect him as he wandered among nomadic tribesmen.

The First Sacrifice: The first sacrifice which was acceptable was that of Abel. He gave an animal (blood) sacrifice. Cain, on the other hand, gave a vegetable sacrifice. Some scholars argue that, although it is not mentioned until later, God expected Cain to know that without a blood sacrifice, sin could not be overlooked. Others are content to say that he did not give God his best, and therefore was jealous of his brother who did. The New Testament (I John 3:12) simply states that Cain was of the evil one, and that he murdered Abel because his own deeds were evil and his brother's righteous.

The First Covenant: The first "covenant" between God and man is the agreement that God would never again destroy the earth by water, the rainbow being the seal or sign of this covenant. The "covenant" is an important motif in the Bible. Christians divide the Bible itself into the Old and the New Covenants. (The word testament means covenant.)

The Curse of Canaan: The story of Noah's curse upon Canaan was used in the seventeenth, eighteenth, and nineteenth centuries to defend the enslavement of Africans. The curse was motivated by Ham's transgression when he looked upon his father Noah's nakedness. Shem and Japheth had, instead, covered their father, with great decorum, during his drunken sleep.

When Noah arose, he blessed Shem and Japheth, and he cursed Ham, but not directly. Rather, he pronounced the curse on one of Ham's sons, Canaan. The children of Israel, under Joshua, later conquered the land of Canaan (Palestine), and the Israelites did indeed subject the Canaanites to slavery, thus fulfilling Noah's curse, which advocates of black African slavery failed to note. They argued that since the curse was on Ham (which, we have seen, was not the case) and that since Ham was the father of Cush, Egypt, and Put, all African nations, then the curse of servitude must be the lot of the African.

The Flood: Controversy still rages among scholars as to whether the flood was or was not universal. Many argue that a flood occurred which inundated only the Near East, while others insist on the veracity of the biblical text that it covered the whole world.

That some kind of major flood occurred in ancient times is not particularly disputed. Archaeological discoveries of flood layers in the strata of ancient cities, e.g., Ur and Kish, combined with literary traditions of ancient peoples telling of a catastrophic flood, have silenced most controversy in this area.

In the nineteenth century, Babylonian tablet inscriptions were discovered that relate a flood story remarkably similar to that of Genesis. In it, a man named Utnapishtim tells how he was warned by the gods to build an ark for the flood they would be sending to destroy mankind. His story is part of the Gilgamesh epic. For further information, consult the works listed in the bibliography.

THE TOWER OF BABEL (Gen. 11:1-9)

1. What significant point about language is made in verse 1?
2. What caused the men to try to build a tower to reach the sky?
3. What was God's reason for confounding their languages?
4. To what two questions that have puzzled mankind does this story provide an answer?

THE CALL OF ABRAHAM (Gen. 12:1-13:13)

Every Jew can trace his lineage back to Abraham, the "Patriarch of Faith," who lived somewhere between 2200 and 2000 B.C. He was descended from Shem, but his father Terah worshiped other gods, according to Joshua 24:2.

1. Why did God call Abraham rather than someone else? Is it possible that God called many other people who didn't respond to his call?
2. What three important promises did God make to Abraham if he would leave his own country for a strange land?
3. Why does the Bible include the account of Abraham's "half lie" about his wife being his sister?
4. How does Abraham demonstrate his faith in the conflict with his nephew Lot?
5. Why did Lot choose Sodom rather than Canaan?
6. Abraham means "father of many nations." Explain the significance of this name.

God Requires Faith: Notice that Abraham was asked to demonstrate his faith twice. First, he was asked to journey into an unknown land, even though he was a very rich man, and had a comfortable situation where he lived. Later, he had to decide whether to demand the preferable land of the Jordan Valley for himself, or to give Lot the first choice. (Abraham didn't have to let Lot choose, because the elder had the option.)

Human Frailty: Popular folklore, religious and secular, generally demands that its heroes be faultless, exhibiting all the qualities of courage, wit, strength, wisdom, and fidelity that we so often lack. This demand has produced the Hollywood film-idol and his cynical counterpart, the anti-hero of the new pornography, who is so perverse, he is utterly devoid of every positive quality. In this way, the anti-hero remains strictly within the genre of the film-idol — both are basically unreal.

The Bible is generally unresponsive to such demands, depicting its heroes with a surprising frankness. Abraham's capacity for falsehood and cowardliness (seen when he masquerades as his wife's brother, allowing her to be violated by local princes) may disappoint an idol-seeker, but it will strike a responsive chord in the heart of one who hungers for reality.

The Chosen People: William Ewer once quipped, "How odd of God to choose the Jews." And one often wonders what led to the selection of this little nation whose impact on the entire world has been so out of proportion to its size. In the call of Abraham, we are at a critical juncture in the selective process. Abraham was descended from Shem, who had received the blessing of Noah, a "preacher of righteousness." Yet the succeeding generations seem to have dimmed that rich awareness of God — Terah, Abram's father, was an idolater. When God called, would Abram respond? God had to find faith in the one he would choose, and so Abram's exercise of belief or unbelief would be the key to unlock or lock the door into the next stage of history. The key turned, and the door swung open, as we read in Genesis 15:6 (RSV): "And he believed the Lord; and he reckoned it to him as righteousness." Such is the background of "the chosen people."

The return of the Jews to Palestine in 1947 for the establishment of an autonomous state is regarded by many as part of the fulfillment of God's promise to Abraham. This is a disputed point, but it is not insignificant that after wandering among the nations of the Gentiles for nearly two millennia, Israel is once again a member of the family of nations—a thing unparalleled in the world's history.

Some scholars regard Abraham as a legendary figure with little or no historical reality, but it is fair to say that these scholars are in the minority. The stories of Genesis are, of course, the strongest evidence for his existence, but there is also considerable archaeological evidence that would favor a historical interpretation of Abraham and history.

THE DESTRUCTION OF SODOM AND GOMORRAH
(Gen. 18:16–19:26)

1. Why did God want to destroy Sodom and Gomorrah?
2. How was Abraham able to persuade God to spare the city, and why was it destroyed after all?
3. What does the destruction of Sodom and Gomorrah tell us about the personality of God? Has this attribute of God come up before in our reading? Where?
4. What did the men of the city want with the men (angels) visiting Lot?
5. How does the word "sodomy" originate from this story?
6. Why was Lot's wife turned into a pillar of salt? What did her looking back really mean? What biblical principle does this punishment illustrate?

Sodomy: The word sodomy, which means sex perversion, originated with this story when the men of Sodom wanted to "know" (have sexual intercourse with) the angels visiting Lot.

They were more interested in the men (angels) than in Lot's daughters, whom he offered in place of the angels.

Looking Back: The biblical warning against looking back with longing toward that which one has left behind is supremely illustrated by Lot's wife. She disobeyed God's instructions for the time when his wrath was to be poured out, and so was caught in that outpouring. The instructions had been designed to keep them safe from that fury of fire and brimstone. Jesus warned his disciples to "remember Lot's wife" (Luke 17:32) when he was teaching them the urgency of fleeing from God's wrath on "the day when the Son of man is revealed." Elsewhere he taught that those who put their hand to the plow, and look back, are not worthy of his kingdom (Luke 9:62). Looking back, then, symbolizes a failure to take God's anger against evil seriously — it is the act of what the Bible calls a scoffer (Ps. 1:1 RSV).

THE PROMISE OF AN HEIR FOR ABRAHAM
(Gen. 16:1–18:15; 21–22)

1. Which promise was Abraham attempting to fulfill when he fathered a child by Hagar?
2. How do you know that God was not pleased with this method of fulfillment? Contrast God's way of fulfilling the promise with Abraham's way.
3. What is the purpose of God's talk with Abraham in chapter 17, and what is the seal of the agreement or covenant?
4. Why is "laughter" (the meaning, in Hebrew, of "Isaac") a good name for Abraham and Sarah's son?
5. What promise is made to Ishmael, even though he is not to be the heir of Abraham?
6. How does Abraham prove that he has learned a lesson in faith when he is asked to sacrifice his son?
7. What other reasons might God have had for asking Abraham to kill his only son Isaac?

Spiritual Growth: That Abraham was ready to slay his only son, the child he had received by a miracle, demonstrates a remarkable change or spiritual growth. The man who was once so full of unbelief (witness: Hagar) is now ready to sacrifice his only visible link to God's promise that he would become a great nation. The scene on that mountain in Moriah is one of the most dramatic in world literature, establishing for all time Abraham's status as *the* man of faith who knew that the Lord would provide.

The Arab Nations: Ishmael, the son of Abraham by Hagar, became the patriarch of the tribe of the Ishmaelites, a term used to describe in general the wandering caravan traders, tent-dwellers, and camel-herders who, living in settlements and nomadic camps, inhabited the desert regions of North Arabia in ancient times (Gen. 25:18).

Today, popular tradition holds that the Arab nations are descended from the twelve sons of Ishmael. It is interesting to note the ferocious enmity of the Arab nations for Israel, and the possibility of still listing the Arab states under twelve names: Lebanon, Syria, Yemen, Jordan, Egypt, Saudi-Arabia, Sudan, Libya, Tunisia, Morocco, Algeria, and Iraq.

The Ram's Horn and Rosh Hashanah: When Abraham was about to lower the knife to kill his son, an angel stopped him. Then he noticed a ram caught in the bushes. God had provided himself with a sacrifice. For this reason, on Rosh Hashanah, the Jewish New Year, a ram's horn is blown in the synagogue. The people recall the faithfulness of God in the most hopeless situations, and gain courage to face the unknown trials of life which may arise in the coming year.

THE CHOSEN FAMILY MULTIPLIES
JACOB GETS THE BIRTHRIGHT
(Gen. 24, 25:19–34; 27)

1. Why was Abraham so concerned about the bloodline of his son Isaac's wife?

2. How does Abraham's servant demonstrate his faith in God in his method of choosing a bride for Isaac?

3. Compare the marriage ceremony of Isaac and Rebekah with the marriage ceremony of today.

4. Why was Esau an unfit person to become an heir to Abraham and an inheritor of the promise?

5. What indication did God give Rebekah at the birth of her sons that Jacob, the youngest, would be the son of promise?

6. How did both Jacob and Rebekah demonstrate lack of faith?

JACOB "REAPS WHAT HE HAS SOWN"
(Gen. 29–33, 35)

1. Jacob "tricked" his brother into selling him the birthright. How is Jacob in turn deceived by Laban? Give two examples. What biblical principle does this illustrate?

2. Name the twelve children of Jacob, listing them according to their mothers.

3. Why are the twelve sons of Jacob vital to Jewish identity, even to this day?

4. Why is Jacob's name finally changed to Israel (which means "He who strives with God")?

5. Why didn't Jacob have trouble with Esau when he returned to his homeland?

Spiritual Growth and Name Change: The critical point of Jacob's spiritual growth was his wrestling match with the angel at the ford of the Jabbok. There the Lord gave him a new name, Israel, signifying the new man he had become during his fourteen years of servitude to Laban. It was then, as a man broken and yet triumphant in his striving with God, that Jacob was ready to meet his brother Esau whom he had so bitterly wronged.

JOSEPH, FROM SHEPHERD TO RULER
(Gen. 37, 39–41)

1. Why was it annoying to Joseph's brothers that Joseph's father gave him a "coat of many colors," and that Joseph had the two dreams? What did all of this seem to be telling them?
2. What good comes, almost immediately, of Joseph's being sold into slavery?
3. How is Joseph's faith tested in Potiphar's house?
4. From a providential point of view, why is Joseph thrown into prison?
5. What position is Joseph given in prison? What does this foreshadow?
6. Describe the four dreams that Joseph interprets. How does this gift from God (of being able to interpret dreams) get him from prison to rulership of Egypt?
7. Explain Joseph's ultimate position in terms of divine providence.

Joseph's Coat: The coat was actually a long robe with sleeves which exalted its wearer above his fellows wearing the more common sleeveless tunic that reached only to the knees. This alone made Joseph's brothers implacably bitter, so that the dreams only added fuel to an already raging fire of hatred.

Leadership: Joseph's capacity for leadership was presaged by his father's gift, and by the dreams he himself dreamed. Once he was in Egypt, his capacity began to be recognized, and he was soon placed over Potiphar's household. When his uprightness toward Potiphar's wife landed him in prison, even there he rose to prominence and was finally brought out of jail to be made the regent of all Egypt under Pharaoh.

Divine Providence: Divine providence is clearly demonstrated in the story of Joseph. Joseph's being sold into Egypt may have seemed a negative thing, yet it was necessary for

Joseph to get to Egypt to become ruler and thus to save the chosen family. Also, had Joseph not been falsely accused by Potiphar's wife, he wouldn't have had the opportunity to interpret the butler's dreams, and thus be remembered before Pharaoh by the butler. The principle of "providence" is reiterated throughout the Old and New Testaments. Paul states (Rom. 8:28) that "all things work together for good to those who love God and are the called according to his purpose."

THE CHOSEN FAMILY SAVED FROM FAMINE
(Gen. 42, 45, 50)

1. Joseph's brothers bow down before him when they come for grain. Relate this to a dream Joseph had. Of what is this an example?
2. Why isn't Joseph eager to take revenge upon the brothers who sold him into slavery?
3. Why does God allow Egypt to prosper in a time of famine?
4. Why is it necessary for Jacob to move with his entire family to Egypt? How has God already prepared the way?

EXODUS

In Greek, the word *exodus* means "going out" — an appropriate title for the book which describes the escape or exit of the Hebrew people from the land of bondage, Egypt.

Most scholars agree that the book is historically based, but differ greatly as to the time of the exodus from Egypt. Valid arguments exist for a wide variety of dates from 1700 to 1200 B.C. The route of the exodus has been substantiated by archeological expeditions which have confirmed the biblical accuracy regarding the topography of the land. Albright (see bibliography) discusses this at length.

Moses is the central human figure of Exodus, standing as God's agent to deliver his people from bondage, as the mediator of the covenant at Sinai, and as the interpreter of the law and of God's redemptive acts. It is in this book that we learn the most about the personality and background of this great leader of Israel.

The departure from Egypt, with the parting of the sea, is the most important event of redemption in the Old Testament. It is recited again and again in the Psalms in celebration of the Lord's saving power (e.g., Ps. 78).

THE ENSLAVEMENT OF THE CHOSEN
(Exod. 1-6)

1. How did Pharaoh plan to control the growth of the Hebrew population?
2. Show how providence was in operation in the life of Moses from the time he was an infant.
3. Prove that Moses identified himself with the Hebrews rather than with the Egyptians.
4. Describe Moses' dramatic experience with God in the desert of Midian. How does this experience affect the rest of his life?
5. List two examples in the life of Moses, prior to his encounter with God, that point to Moses as a deliverer.
6. Explain the meaning of God's name "I Am."
7. What excuses does Moses give God when he is told to deliver the Hebrews? What does this tell us about Moses?
8. What is the purpose of Exodus 6:1-8?

THE PLAGUES AND THE PASSOVER
(Exod. 7-13)

1. By what power did the Egyptian magicians perform the same miracles performed by Moses in 7:10-12?
2. How does Moses show the superiority of God?
3. List the ten plagues. What do they have in common?

4. Explain the origin to the Jewish holiday, "Passover," in terms of the last plague.
5. Relate the "seder" to the events described in Exodus 7–13.
6. In Christian typology, what does the lamb represent?
7. Which of the plagues do you feel would be most difficult to explain as a force of nature?

The Seder: At the Jewish Passover feast, called a "seder" ("order" or "ritual"), Jewish families eat a dinner of special foods. Each food symbolizes an aspect of their enslavement and escape from Egypt.

Typology: Christians believe that the lamb is a type of Christ, since Christ came to redeem mankind from sin and eternal death. The blood of the paschal lamb saved the Jews from the death angel, so the blood of Christ, say the New Testament authors, saves a believer from eternal death (e.g., I John 1:7).

SOME INTERESTING LAWS (Exod. 21–22)

1. In what manner were the Hebrews commanded to treat slaves? Compare this commandment with the treatment of slaves in pre–Civil War America.
2. What was the punishment for cursing one's mother? Why was it so severe?
3. What was the fate of a witch? Why?
4. What was the punishment for lying with a beast?
5. What is said about taking vengeance?
6. What does the law say about the treatment of strangers and widows? What do these laws say about the nature of God?

Witchcraft: See special article in appendix.

LEVITICUS

The worship of Israel is the pre-eminent theme of Leviticus, as it prescribes, sometimes in minute detail, the proper procedure for the animal sacrificial system and the conducting of the great annual feasts which are still practiced today in Judaism and are commonly thought of in America as "Jewish holidays." The name of the book comes from Jerome's Vulgate which was derived from the Septuagint title, *Leueitikon* – that is, the book which deals with the Levitical priests and their duties. The tribe of Levi, of which Moses and Aaron were members, was set apart for the priesthood. In Hebrew, the title is simply the first word of the book, *wayiqra,* "and he called."

THE LEVITICAL ORDINANCES (Lev. 1–5, 10, 17–18)

1. What was the purpose of the burnt offerings in chapters 1–2?
2. What was the purpose of the peace offering (chap. 3)?
3. Under what circumstances was a sin offering made?
4. What special condition was required of each sacrificial animal?
5. Why were Nadab and Abihu killed?
6. Why were the people forbidden to eat blood? (See book by Gaster, listed in the bibliography.)
7. List specifically those with whom marriage is forbidden in chapter 18.

THE JEWISH HOLIDAYS ORDAINED IN LEVITICUS
(Lev. 23–24)

The seven Jewish holidays mentioned in chapters twenty-three and twenty-four are:

1. Weekly Sabbath (23:1–3)
2. Passover (23:5–8)

3. Pentecost (23:10–21) (also known as Shabuoth)
4. Rosh Hashanah (23:24–25) (New Year)
5. Yom Kippur (23:26–32) (Day of Atonement)
6. Sukkoth (23:39–44) (Feast of Booths, or Tabernacles)
7. Perpetual Light (24:1–9) (Shew Bread)

(*The Zondervan Bible Dictionary,* listed in the bibliography, provides detailed information on each of these days. Also see Guthrie and Moyer.)

1. What is the purpose of each of these special days?
2. Which day is the most holy? Why?
3. Which day relates to events recorded in Exodus?

NUMBERS

The book of Numbers derives its name from the first chapter, in which God commands Moses to number or count the people. The events of the book take place during the forty years the Hebrews wandered in the wilderness before entering into the land promised to their forefather Abraham.

SPECIAL CALLS AND PUNISHMENT FOR SIN
(Num. 1, 3, 6, 11–14, 16, 20–21, 27)

1. What is the job (call) of a Levite?
2. What is the special call of a Nazirite?
3. Describe the spiritual condition of the Hebrew people as recorded in chapters 11–14. Contrast their faith with the faith of Abraham.
4. Why do Miriam and Aaron complain against Moses? How and why are they punished?
5. Why does God refuse to allow Moses to enter the promised land? What does this tell you about the nature of God?
6. Why does God send fiery serpents upon the people?
7. Who is chosen to lead the people into the promised land? Who does the choosing?

Moses' Wife: Miriam and Aaron rebelled against Moses' authority because of his marriage to a non-Israelite woman. (Zipporah, his wife, was a Midianite. Apparently the term Cushite, which normally refers to the Sudan, here encompasses a large segment of Arabic peoples.) Moses' great meekness is demonstrated by his unwillingness to defend himself, a virtue rewarded by God himself taking up Moses' cause against the rebels.

The Brazen Serpent: There are three interesting sidelights to the story of the serpent that Moses made of brass and set atop a pole in the middle of the camp to stay the plague of serpents by which God had judged the people (Num. 21:4–9). The statuette was apparently preserved for some time after Moses sculptured it, and it later became an idol named Nehushtan to which the people burnt incense (II Kings 18:4). Much later, Jesus likened Moses' lifting up of the serpent to his own death by being lifted up on a cross so that whoever believed in him might not perish (John 3:14–15). Finally, in the growth of the medical profession from ancient times, this story came to provide the symbol employed to this day to represent the healing science, a serpent coiled around a pole.

DEUTERONOMY

Deuteronomy means "second law," a term applied by the Septuagint based on a misunderstanding of 17:18 which does not refer to a repetition, but to a copy of the law. Its theme is the renewal of the covenant wherein the legal codes of Exodus and Leviticus are re-asserted and freshly interpreted for the peculiarities of a new life situation in Canaan west of the Jordan. The setting of the book is the Israeli encampment in the plains of Moab prior to invasion. Moses must depart the scene before the entrance to the promised land, and this is the opportunity for his farewell discourse. There are actually three addresses in all, 1:6–4:40; 5–28; 29–30, followed by the scenes of Moses' death and preparation for invasion, chapters 31–34.

A unique element in Deuteronomy is the instruction that worship was to be conducted in one central shrine, thus eliminating the pagan practice of many local altars (chap. 12).

THE RENEWAL OF THE COVENANT
(Deut. 3:23–28; 4; 6:4–9; 14:22–29; 22–24; 31; 34)

1. What insight into God's personality do you gain by the conversation between God and Moses in 3:23–38?
2. What does God warn the Israelites will happen to them if they neglect to obey his commandments?
3. Deuteronomy 6:4–9 is known as the "Shema." ("Shema" is the Hebrew word meaning "Hear.") What is the main point of that passage, and why was it extremely important in its historical context? Why is it still held most sacred by religious Jews?
4. Explain the origin of "tithe giving," using Deuteronomy 14:22–29.
5. What is transvestism, and what does Deuteronomy say about it?
6. Explain chapter 31 in terms of your own view of prophecy.
7. Give your own explanation for Moses not being withered and blind, even though he was quite old. What do you think the biblical explanation is? (Compare Ps. 1:2–3.)

Special Project: The Ten Commandments

Study the Ten Commandments carefully and give your opinion pro or con as to their relevance in 20th century life. Exodus 20:1–17; Deuteronomy 5:6–21.

The Historical Books

The second section of the Old Testament surveys the history of the people of Israel from the beginning of the conquest of Canaan under Joshua (*ca.* 1350 B.C.) until the post-exilic era when Judah was a part of the Persian empire. The story, though marked throughout with events of triumph, is one of overall decline as the nation drifted further and further from the God who called Abraham out of Ur.

After the reign of Solomon, probably the era of Israel's greatest splendor, the nation was divided into two kingdoms. The northern kingdom, commonly called Israel, fell prey to Assyrian expansion, its capital city, Samaria, capitulating to siege in 722 B.C. One hundred and fifty years later, Jerusalem, capital of the southern kingdom (Judah), collapsed before the onslaughts of Nebuchadnezzar, who deported most of the inhabitants to Babylon (the Babylonian captivity). However, within seventy years, the Jews were returning from that exile to the homeland. The Persians under Cyrus had achieved domination of the old Babylonian empire, and an edict was issued that authorized the Jews to return to Jerusalem (539 B.C.).

From that point, the great objective was the rebuilding of the Temple that had been destroyed in 587. The Second Temple, as it came to be known, was completed in 515 B.C. The historical books apparently record no events after 400 B.C., the beginning of the inter-testamental period.

The historical books are Joshua, Judges, Ruth, I and II Samuel, I and II Kings, I and II Chronicles, Ezra, Nehemiah, and Esther.

JOSHUA

After wandering between Egypt and Palestine for forty years, the twelve tribes were finally ready for the invasion of Canaan. Joshua had already been selected to succeed Moses (Num. 27:12–23) primarily because of his faithfulness in reporting his positive conclusions after the reconnaissance mission that Moses had dispatched into Canaan many years before. Of all the men in that mission, only Joshua and Caleb expressed faith that God would open the land to the people by subduing the present inhabitants. The others complained of giants in the land and were certain that any invasion would be suicidal (Num. 13:1–14:10). Now Joshua and Caleb were the only survivors of that generation who would see the beginning of the conquest of Canaan.

The first objective after crossing the Jordan was the walled city of Jericho. The successive battles at Ai and elsewhere report the breaking of Canaanite power throughout the whole land. The second half of the book, chapters 13–23, describes the various tribal allotments in the newly gained real estate.

THE CONQUEST OF CANAAN
(Josh. 1–2, 6–7, 20, 24)

1. What promise did God give to Joshua?
2. How did Rahab know that the spies were sent by God?
3. What was Rahab's reward? What was her profession, and why is it important to the account?
4. What unconventional thing did God have the Israelite soldiers do to capture Jericho and why?
5. What was Achan's sin and punishment?
6. What does the provision of cities of refuge tell you about the character of God?
7. What important thing does Joshua do for the people before he dies, and how do the people respond?

JUDGES

The closest thing in the Bible to an American western, the Book of Judges relates the often colorful and occasionally gory events of Israel's history from the death of Joshua until the time of the prophet Samuel. It was a time of lawlessness and corruption when, according to the unknown author-compiler, "every man did what was right in his own eyes" (17:6 RSV) because "there was no king in Israel" (18:1; 19:1; 21:25).

The judges after whom the book is named were actually a succession of thirteen leaders noted usually for their military prowess and sometimes for their sage advice. The most notable ones, Deborah, Gideon, and Samson, were of the military sort, their daring exploits making some of the most exciting reading to be had in all the Bible. The author's primary purpose in telling their stories is to emphasize the doctrine that God blesses his people when they are faithful to him and sends judgment when they are disobedient.

The thirteen judges of Israel were:

1. Othniel, 3:7–11.
2. Ehud, 3:15–30.
3. Shamgar, 3:31.
4. Deborah, 4:1–5:31.
5. Gideon, 6:11–8:35.
6. Abimelech, 9:1–54.
7. Tola, 10:1–2.
8. Jair, 10:3–5.
9. Jephthah, 11:1–12:7.
10. Ibzan, 12:8–10.
11. Elon, 12:11–12.
12. Abdon, 12:13–15.
13. Samson, 13:1–16:31.

THE FIRST JUDGES (Judg. 1–6)

1. In what way do the Israelite tribes disobey the command of God in chapter 1, and what are the consequences in chapter 2?
2. When did God characteristically raise up a judge to save the people from oppression?
3. What does Deborah's role as a military leader tell us about God's view of women?
4. In her "Song" of chapter 5, Deborah refers to herself as a "mother in Israel." Why is this an appropriate title for her?
5. Jael is also a heroine in chapters 4–5. What is her heroic deed?
6. Why was it so difficult for Gideon to believe that God wanted him to deliver the Israelites from their enemies?
7. Explain the episode of Gideon's fleece. What purpose did it serve? Construct a modern-day "fleece."
8. What does God's willingness to go along with Gideon and his many "tests" tell us about God's relationship to man?

THE STORY OF SAMSON (Judg. 13–16)

Samson was under the Nazirite vow, which meant that he was separated unto God and could neither drink strong drink, nor cut his hair. (For the full conditions of a Nazirite vow, see Numbers 6:1–21).

1. What was miraculous about the birth of Samson? List any similar miraculous births studied thus far.
2. What prophecy did the angel of God make concerning Samson, even before Samson was born?
3. Samson's attitude about marrying the Philistine woman points up a possible "Achilles' heel" in him. What is it?
4. How does Delilah get Samson to tell her the secret of his strength? Relate this to his fault.

5. Explain, in accordance with your own beliefs and philosophy, the killing of one thousand men with the jawbone of an ass (15:15–16).
6. What biblical principle is demonstrated in the life of Samson?

RUTH

The poignant warmth of the Book of Ruth has enchanted readers of every generation, giving, as it does, an intimate vignette of the life of the common people in the days of the Judges. Unlike the bloody and violent tales of the Book of Judges, this is the tender story of a young Moabite woman and how her compassion for her widowed mother-in-law later brought her into matrimony with a wealthy man.

When reading this tale, it is important to remember that Moabites were among those forbidden to enter the assembly of the Lord (Deut. 23:3). They were hated enemies of Israel, and for Ruth to adopt as her own the God of Israel was a significant act of conversion. Undoubtedly the author, who remains anonymous, wanted to make a theological point in addition to telling a charming story. Ruth became the great-grandmother of David, progenitor of Solomon and all the kings of Judah. The point is that God, by allowing a Gentile such an important position, demonstrated greater concern about inner qualities of faith and devotion than about outward matters of pedigree.

In the Hebrew canon, the Book of Ruth is included among the "rolls" and is read in the synagogue annually on Shabuoth (Pentecost), the feast that commemorates the giving of the Law at Mount Sinai and which marked the beginning of the offering of the first fruits of the harvest. It is this harvest celebration in the Book of Ruth that is the occasion of her betrothal to Boaz (chap. 3).

THE ROMANCE OF RUTH (Ruth 1–4)

1. In chapter 1, both Ruth and her sister-in-law, Orpah, offer to return with their mother-in-law, Naomi, to Israel. How does the old woman try to discourage them from accompanying her?
2. What does Ruth's response to Naomi (1:16–17) reveal about Ruth's character?
3. To what city in Israel do they return?
4. Describe the process of gleaning in agriculture.
5. What is a threshing floor?
6. Explain the events of chapters 3 and 4 in light of Deuteronomy 25:5–6.
7. What is the point of the genealogy in 4:18–22?

Kinsman – Redemption: Notice that the child that Ruth bore to Boaz was given to Naomi, who nursed the infant. In effect, the child became her own and was named Obed (servant) to celebrate the old woman's deliverance from desolation. The ancient law (compare Gen. 38:6–11 with Deut. 25:5–10) provided that if a man died, then his nearest of kin would take the widow as his own. Any children to emerge from this arrangement were regarded as the offspring of the deceased man, so that his name would not be blotted out. Of course Naomi was a double widow in that her husband and her sons had died, leaving no progeny. Her widowed daughter-in-law, Ruth, by her willingness to receive Naomi's God and his law that her child would be as much Naomi's as her own, became the instrument of her mother-in-law's salvation.

I SAMUEL

The books of I and II Samuel were originally one piece in Hebrew, having been divided in two simply to produce a book of more manageable size (see The Old Testament, pp. 29–30). They are by far the most vividly written historical documents of the entire Old Testament, pointing to an author (he is anonymous) who was an eyewitness of the events he records with such sensitivity and perception. The great drama of I Samuel is the tumultuous relationship between David and Saul. The book begins with the birth of the great prophet Samuel, who became the agonized father of the Israelite monarchy. He first anointed the handsome Saul to be king, but was later forced to reject him in favor of David.

THE BIRTH AND CALL OF SAMUEL
THE ARK OF GOD
(I Sam. 1–7)

1. What is miraculous about the birth of Samuel? Compare his birth with those of Isaac and Samson.
2. Describe the call of Samuel. Why was such a call necessary?
3. When the Philistines took the ark of God, their own god, Dagon, was found fallen on its face. What does this signify?

The Philistines: The Philistines, the perennial enemies of Israel, occupied a strip of land on the Mediterranean coast southwest of Jerusalem, roughly equivalent to the modern-day Gaza Strip. They were a people whose origin was hidden in the mists of history. Jeremiah called them "the remnant of the coastland of Caphtor" (Jer. 47:4 RSV), but no one is certain where Caphtor was. It probably referred generally to the whole area of the Aegean Sea between Greece and Asia Minor.

Philistia was a fertile plain, though threatened by sand dunes from the south, and it was apparently through commercial contact with the people of this prosperous coastal plain that the Greeks became familiar with the region south of Lebanon (Tyre and Sidon) and began to call it "Palestine" after the Philistines. Philistia supported five major cities. Gaza,

Ashkelon, and Ashdod were on the coast, Gath and Ekron a few miles inland.

Stories of giants were common to the whole district, stemming back in the biblical tradition to a certain Anak of whom it was said, "Who can stand before the sons of Anak?" (Deut. 9:2 RSV). Goliath was from Gath and was reported to be about ten feet tall (I Sam. 17:4). These giants apparently resided side-by-side with the more normally tall Philistines as a remnant of their ancient tribes.

Little is known of the actual practices of Philistine religion. Temples of Dagon, a god with the hands and face of a man and the body of a fish, existed in Gaza and Ashdod (Judg. 16:23; I Sam. 5:1-7). Ashkelon, according to the Greek historian Herodotus (I, 105), had a temple to the fertility goddess Ashtoreth, and Baalzebub was honored in Ekron (II Kings 1:1-16). A temple to Dagon is reported in Ashdod long after the destruction of the Philistine race (I Macc. 10:83). In Isaiah's time, the Philistines had a reputation for soothsaying (Isa. 2:6).

The most famous biblical reference to these pagan neighbors of Israel came from the mouth of David who asked, upon hearing of Goliath, "Who is this uncircumcised Philistine, that he should defy the armies of the living God?" (I Sam. 17:26). The constant antagonism between Israel and Philistia was put to use in the nineteenth century by Matthew Arnold, the famous British poet and writer, in his book *Culture and Anarchy,* where he defined a Philistine as one who believed in and worshiped material prosperity, disregarding cultural, esthetic, and spiritual values whether out of ignorance or smug indifference.

THE PEOPLE DEMAND A KING
SAUL IS ANOINTED
SAUL SINS AGAINST GOD
(I Sam. 8-10, 15)

1. Why did the elders of Israel want to have a king, and how did God feel about this? Why did God feel this way?

2. How did Saul know that he was the one chosen of God to be the king of Israel? Why did God allow him this method of knowing?
3. How does Saul disobey God in the war with Amalek? What does this disobedience foreshadow?
4. First Samuel 15:22 says, "To obey is better than sacrifice, and to hearken than the fat of rams." Explain this quotation, and relate it to the biblical principle of obedience.

The Amalekites: The Amalekites were a nomadic people who were the first to attack the Israelites on their way to the promised land (Exod. 17:8–16). God commanded the Israelites to utterly destroy them (I Sam. 15:1–3).

SAMUEL ANOINTS DAVID AS KING
DAVID SLAYS GOLIATH
SAUL TRIES TO KILL DAVID
(I Sam. 16–21)

1. Why is it surprising that David was chosen above Jesse's other sons? Can you think of a similar example already studied?
2. What was bothering King Saul in 16:14?
3. How does David comfort Saul?
4. How does David's killing of Goliath function to bring about David's eventual kingship? Explain this in terms of divine providence.
5. What is the significance of David's eating the holy bread which was reserved only for the priests?
6. Why does Saul want to kill David?

THE RESPECT FOR GOD'S ANOINTED
THE WITCH OF ENDOR
(I Sam. 24, 28, 31)

1. Why is David kind to Saul in spite of all that Saul has done to harm him?

2. Why has Saul put an end to all witches and wizards?
3. Why does Saul resort to a visit to a witch?
4. What did Saul hope to hear from the prophet Samuel, and what does he hear? Why does God allow him to learn this?
5. Why won't Saul's armor bearer kill him?

God's Anointed: David's behavior toward his enemy Saul is quite puzzling to the modern reader. Even when David had Saul's life in his grasp, he refused to "touch the Lord's anointed." Recall that when Samuel pronounced the coronation of Saul as king, the act was accomplished by pouring oil over Saul's head. This was "anointing" a person to be king and signified an enduement from the Spirit of God of the right to exercise authority over God's people. The anointed person represented God himself in a mysterious and awesome way. One who wished to please God would always treat the Lord's anointed with the utmost respect, even if the Lord's anointed had himself been disobedient to God and incurred God's wrath as Saul had.

David seems to have believed that God was so powerful and sovereign that he could use Saul, even in his disobedient state, to represent God to David in a backhanded sort of way. When Saul sought to murder David, David saw it as something that drove him closer to God for safety. David, while eluding Saul, treated him with reverence. While modern man might disdain such behavior, the Bible implies that God was quite pleased with David because of it and rewarded him accordingly.

Note also that, even in the moment of Saul's death, Saul's armor bearer seems to have been aware of this principle, as he refused to touch Saul even to put him out of his misery.

Necromancy: The raising of the spirits of the dead is called necromancy. The attempt to raise such spirits usually takes place at a seance. Many biblical scholars argue that the devil cannot bring up the actual spirit of a dead person, but only an imitation of it. Others argue that he can, but that the spirit is subject to God, as in this case. (See appendix article, "Witchcraft.")

II SAMUEL

In II Samuel, David consolidates and strengthens the kingdom. He brings the ark of God to Jerusalem and establishes that city as the spiritual and political center of Israel. He extends the territory to its furthest point in Hebrew history. Finally, David sins against God in the matter of Bathsheba, and is punished by civil war and foreign attack for the remainder of his reign.

Many scholars date the reign of David from 1010 to 970 B.C.

THE EXPLOITS AND FAILINGS OF KING DAVID
(II Sam. 3, 6–7, 11–12, 19, 22)

1. What is the significance of David bringing the ark of God into Jerusalem?
2. Why does David want to build a temple, and why is he denied the privilege?
3. What is the double sin of David, and how does God rebuke him for it through Nathan the prophet?
4. Explain Nathan's parable.
5. What is David's punishment?
6. Prove through a biblical reference that David, in spite of his punishment, has not lost his faith in God.

I AND II KINGS

The Books of the Kings cover the period from the last days of King David to the Babylonian captivity (977 to 586 B.C.). First Kings tells of the life of King Solomon and the building of the Temple. Upon Solomon's death, the nation divides into two kingdoms, the northern kingdom of Israel and the southern kingdom of Judah. Israel consists of ten tribes, and Judah of two (Benjamin and Judah.)

Second Kings tells how the northern kingdom of Israel was

taken over by Assyria, and its inhabitants were taken into captivity. (Today, these ten tribes are often referred to as the "ten lost tribes" of Israel.) One hundred thirty-five years after the downfall of the northern kingdom, the southern kingdom of Judah was taken captive by Babylonia.

The Books of the Kings are traditionally assigned to Jeremiah (as editor), since his career dovetailed precisely with the end of the Kings' narrative. Some scholars, however, think that there were many men involved in the editing of Kings, and some scholars think that Kings was written at a date much later than the events described in the final chapters of the book.

Whoever the author or authors were, their intent in writing the book is easy to see. They want the reader to see the fulfillment of the Deuteronomic code in Israel's history. Evil kings are punished and righteous kings rewarded. The greater unrighteousness was committed in the northern kingdom, since the founder of that kingdom, Jeroboam the son of Nebat, committed apostasy from the first by refusing to worship at Jerusalem and establishing his own priesthood and places of worship. The overall picture is one of general decline in both kingdoms until they are finally given over to the will of their enemies.

Many archeological excavations have proved the accuracy of details mentioned in Kings. A cuneiform inscription (now in the British Museum) describes King Ahab's war with other Syrian kings against the Assyrian ruler Shalmaneser III. The tablet provides scholars with an extra-biblical record of a biblical story that can be used for correlation and date-fixing. The battle took place in June, 835 B.C. at Karkar. A black obelisk, also in the British Museum, pictures Jehu (a Hebrew king) prostrate before an Assyrian king. (See Tenney, Albright, and Abbott in the bibliography.)

SOLOMON BECOMES KING
SOLOMON OBTAINS WISDOM AND
BUILDS A TEMPLE FOR GOD
(I Kings 1-8)

1. What does the anointing of King Solomon symbolize?
2. When Solomon has a chance to ask God for anything he wants, he asks for wisdom. What did God give him, and why?
3. How does Solomon prove his wisdom when two mothers come to him with a problem?
4. Contrast the reign of Solomon as described in chapters 4, 5, and 7 with the reign of King David, his father.
5. Why did Solomon want to build a temple for God?
6. What was contained in the Ark of the Covenant?
7. Why were tools of iron and metal forbidden in building the Temple?
8. What symbolized God's presence in and blessing upon the Temple after it was completed? Where else in the Bible did you encounter this symbol for the presence of God?

THE QUEEN OF SHEBA VISITS SOLOMON
THE KINGDOM IS DIVIDED
ELIJAH AND THE BAAL WORSHIPERS
(I Kings 9-12, 16:29-18)

1. What promise and warning does God give to Solomon in chapter 9?
2. What impression did King Solomon make upon the Queen of Sheba?
3. How many chariots and horsemen did Solomon have? Do you think the description is an exaggeration?
4. What is Solomon's sin in chapter 11?

5. What prophecy (chap. 9) is fulfilled as a punishment for Solomon's sin?
6. How does Rehoboam unwittingly help to bring about the division of the kingdom?
7. Describe the morality of Ahab and Jezebel.
8. How did Elijah survive during the drought?
9. What did the widow do for Elijah, and how was she rewarded? In what way did she demonstrate faith?
10. How does Elijah prove the supremacy of his God in a contest with the Baal worshipers?

The Queen of Sheba: The Queen of Sheba ruled a dominion in the southwest portion of the Arabian peninsula. Today, the King of Ethiopia claims to be descended from Solomon and the Queen of Sheba.

Elijah: Elijah holds the highest place amongst the Old Testament prophets, in the minds of Jewish people. He is regarded as the "messenger of good tidings." It is Elijah who is expected to announce the coming of the Messiah, and the redemption of the Jewish people. A place is set for Elijah at the Passover Seder. Folklore pictures him in heaven recording all marriages, and he is said to appear on earth from time to time in order to help needy individuals.

THE LORD ANSWERS ELIJAH IN A SMALL VOICE
NABOTH'S VINEYARD TAKEN BY AHAB
(I Kings 19, 21)

1. Why is Elijah forced to run away?
2. How does Elijah *expect* God to speak to him, and how *does* God speak to him? What is the significance of the manner in which God chooses to speak to Elijah?
3. Who took Elijah's place as a prophet?
4. How does Jezebel manage to get Naboth's vineyard for her husband Ahab?

5. How does her method of obtaining the vineyard demonstrate her extreme cruelty?
6. What prophecy does Elijah deliver concerning Ahab's death? How does Ahab escape this punishment?

God Speaks: The manner in which God chooses to speak to Elijah demonstrates an important biblical concept that God reveals himself in unexpected ways. In this case, Elijah expects to hear from God in a mighty way (wind or earthquake), while, in fact, God speaks to him in a small voice.

ELISHA'S MINISTRY
NAAMAN'S CURE
THE THREAT OF SYRIA
THE FALL OF THE NORTHERN KINGDOM
(II Kings 2, 4–5, 12–13, 17–19)

1. What did Elisha have to do in order to receive a double portion of Elijah's ministry?
2. List three miracles performed by Elisha.
3. How did Naaman demonstrate the biblical principle that faith is a necessary prerequisite for a miracle?
4. How did Joash (Jehoash) show that he really cared about God?
5. Who was the constant enemy of the Hebrew people?
6. Why did God allow Israel to be defeated by the Assyrians?
7. Describe the reign of Hezekiah.
8. What prophecy does Isaiah utter in chapter 19?

MANASSEH'S EVIL REIGN
JOSIAH'S REFORM
THE FALL OF JERUSALEM
(II Kings 21–25)

1. What was Manasseh's main sin?
2. What prompted Josiah's reform?

3. What were the specific reforms instituted by Josiah?
4. How was Josiah different from all the other kings?
5. Explain the ultimate fall of Jerusalem in terms of biblical prophecy.

I AND II CHRONICLES

Chronicles covers the period from the reign of Saul to the return from exile. Much of the material duplicates that of Samuel and Kings. There is, however, a marked difference in emphasis in Chronicles. Chronicles emphasizes the positive aspects of Hebrew history, noting, for example, the many God-given victories of the Hebrews (see II Chron. 13, 20, 25).

Tradition holds that Ezra wrote the beginning of Chronicles, and Nehemiah completed it. Since Ezra was a scribe, he constantly mentions his source materials in the text. Some scholars disagree with an Ezra-Nehemiah authorship, arguing that Chronicles must have been written in 300 B.C. to glorify Hebrew history. No one has come up with conclusive evidence either way, so one is left to examine the evidence for himself and make his own decision. (See Tenney and *Interpreter's Bible* listed in the bibliography.)

THE WORK OF THE CHRONICLER
(I Chron. 9, 16, 22; II Chron. 17, 19–20)

1. Why did the author bother to list the genealogy of the Israelites?
2. What is the main point of the song of praise of David in I Chronicles 16:8–36? What insight into the success of the Israelites does this psalm give?
3. What did David stress in his instructions to his son Solomon, and why did he stress this?
4. After reading the above references in II Chronicles, tell what great thing God did for Jehoshaphat, and why he did it.

5. Why does the author of Chronicles emphasize the positive aspects of Hebrew history rather than the negative aspects? What effect would a reading of Chronicles have upon young men living in the days Chronicles were written?
6. List five negative aspects of Hebrew history by recalling events described in I and II Samuel and I and II Kings.

Ezra

The book of Ezra is named for the main character in the book, who is also its traditional author. Modern scholars, however, think that Ezra, along with the Chronicles and Nehemiah were written (edited) by someone they call "the Chronicler." They believe that Ezra was written between 400 and 300 B.C. (a good deal later than the time of Ezra, who returned to Jerusalem in 458 B.C.).

The book continues the narrative of Chronicles, describing the return of the captives and the rebuilding of the Temple in 536 B.C. It continues to the return of Ezra to Jerusalem, in 458 B.C., to carry out his religious reforms.

Although the Jews had returned from exile, they were not free. They were subjects of the Persian Empire, and were forced to pay tribute to it. The Jews did not have an easy life, as their many enemies continued to harass them, attempting to bring them into disfavor with Persian authorities.

The remaining Israelites were the two tribes of the southern kingdom of Judah (Judah and Benjamin). From this point in history, the designation "Jew" (shortened from Judah) became increasingly common, until all people of Hebrew descent became known as Jews. The Jews, then, were first Hebrews, then Israelites, and finally, Jews.

THE REBULDING OF THE TEMPLE
SINS AND REPENTANCE OF THE JEWS
(Ezra 1, 3-7, 9-10)

1. Why did Cyrus allow the Jews to return to Jerusalem to rebuild the Temple?
2. Why was it so important to the Jews to rebuild the Temple?
3. Why were the Jews forced to stop work on the Temple, and why were they soon able to resume work?
4. What sin did the Levites and priests commit?
5. What did Ezra do about the sins of the people?
6. How did the people react to Ezra's attempt to reform them?

Samaritans: The Samaritans were the main enemies of the Jews in their attempt to rebuild the Temple. According to II Kings 17, they were from Babylon and other parts of Assyria, and had mixed in marriage with Jews from the northern kingdom. They worshiped both God and graven images. The Jews rejected their help, knowing of their pagan tendencies. They then became outraged, and hindered the Jews in every way possible, effecting a work stoppage on the Temple for nine years. The antipathy between the Jews and the Samaritans, so evident in the New Testament, stems from this period of their history.

NEHEMIAH

Ezra is traditionally given credit for having written the Book of Nehemiah. The same arguments are advanced by scholars for this book's authorship as for Ezra and the Chronicles. (See the introductory discussion concerning Ezra.)

The Book of Nehemiah continues the narrative of Ezra. It takes place between 444 and 420 B.C. Nehemiah institutes religious reforms, and oversees the building of the wall of

Jerusalem, in spite of the continued opposition of Sanballat and other Samaritan enemies.

Among the reforms instituted by Nehemiah was the teaching of the law of Moses at the Feast of Tabernacles, as commanded in Deuteronomy 31:10–11. He also initiated a prayer of confession and a renewed promise on the part of the people to return to following their God in accordance with his law.

THE REBUILDING OF THE WALL
THE REFORMS OF NEHEMIAH
(Neh. 1–2, 4, 9–10, 13)

1. On what basis did Nehemiah appeal to God in chapter 1? Of what did he remind God?
2. How did Nehemiah get permission to return to Judah in order to rebuild the wall? Explain this in terms of the biblical principle of "divine providence."
3. Why did Sanballat become angry with Nehemiah, and what plan did he devise? How did the Jews overcome his plan?
4. Why did the people read the entire law of Moses after the wall was completed?
5. Why did the Jews review their entire history in their prayer of repentance to God?
6. What correction was made regarding the keeping of the Sabbath?
7. What warning was issued concerning mixed marriages?

ESTHER

Esther stands in a somewhat unique position among the Old Testament books. The name of God is never mentioned between its covers, nor are any of the usual central matters of Old Testament religion, *e.g.*, Esther's fasting is not accompanied by prayer. For this reason, its place among the other books of the canon was long disputed by the rabbis.

The story is set in the ancient Persian Empire during the

reign of King Ahasuerus. It tells of the deliverance of the Jews from a terrible pogrom planned by the king's wicked prime minister, Haman, who, in the end, is hanged on the very gallows he had built to execute the Jew Mordecai. The scroll of Esther is read for the annual feast of Purim, the only festival in Judaism not prescribed in the Torah. The name "Purim" refers to the lots which Haman cast day after day to ascertain the correct day for his plan of persecution (*Pur* is an Akkadian word meaning "lot").

Many scholars regard Esther as a legendary story, although others point to external evidence of a certain Marduka (whom they equate with Mordecai, Esther's cousin) who held an official post at the capital city of Susa under Xerxes I (Ahasuerus).

THE STORY OF ESTHER
(Esther 1–10)

1. Explain Esther's promotion, as well as the fall of Vashti, in terms of divine providence. At what point in the story does Esther begin to be aware of this providence?
2. Why did Haman hate Mordecai?
3. Explain the timing of the discovery of Mordecai's good deed in terms of divine providence.
4. What example does this story provide of "irony" or "poetic justice"?
5. How does Mordecai help Esther recognize divine providence?
6. Explain the origin of Purim from the narrative of Esther.

Purim: Purim is celebrated in memory of this account. Jews consider the story of Esther to be a classic example of God's victory for his people over their oppressors and take courage from the outcome of events. On Purim (which falls sometime in March), in the synagogue, the Book of Esther is read, and the children twirl their noisemakers (*gragers*) every time the name Haman is read, to drown out his name.

The Poetical Books

The poetry of Israel is a window into the soul of a nation. It expresses every aspect of human emotion, ranging from the furious plea of the psalmist that God would break the teeth of his enemy to the sublime piety of the writer whose soul is quieted as a child is quieted at its mother's breast.

The common form of Hebrew poetry does not involve the rhyme and meter to which we are accustomed in English, as in Marvell's

> But at my back I always hear
> Time's wingèd chariot hurrying near.

Instead, ancient Semitic poetry employed parallelism, in which the same idea is expressed in two slightly different ways, as in Psalm 19:

> The heavens declare the glory of God;
> and the firmament sheweth his handywork.

This feature is an important advantage in the work of translation, since it is nearly impossible to reproduce the rhyme and meter of one language's poetry in another language. Ideas, however, can be translated with reasonable success, thus allowing the parallel structure of Hebrew poetry to stand intact in English translation.

There are elements of Oriental poetry that do not come through in translation, the most notable being the use of acrostic. The acrostic is a composition, usually in verse, in which certain letters (frequently the first in each line), read in order, form a name, title, motto, etc. Hebrew acrostic is invariably alphabetic, in which the initial letters of the lines, or stanzas, are made to run over the letters of the alphabet in their order. Twelve of the psalms contain examples of acrostic.

The poetical books of the Bible are Job, Psalms, Proverbs, Ecclesiastes, and the Song of Solomon.

JOB

The Book of Job is one of the best-known books of the Bible. Dealing with the question of human suffering, especially the suffering of those who are morally upright, its central purpose is to probe the phenomenon of faith in the midst of anguish, in this case, prolonged anguish. It is a powerful, enigmatic masterpiece that has perplexed and absorbed men of every generation.

The name Job (Hebrew *Iyyōbh*) was fairly common among Western Semites in the second millennium B.C., and scholars speculate that the land of Uz meant Edom or perhaps a more northern part of the Transjordan. There is authentic patriarchal coloring in the setting of Job's story: the Aaronic and Levitical priesthoods are absent, wealth is measured in cattle and slaves, the Sabeans and Chaldeans are still depicted as wandering nomads, Job's longevity is reminiscent of the pre-Mosaic era, and the unit of money in 42:11 (Hebrew *qesitah*) is mentioned elsewhere only in Genesis (33:19) and Joshua (24:32).

For these reasons, the ancients assumed that the author was Moses himself, and that Job could perhaps be identified with Jobab, king of Edom (Gen. 36:33) and grandson of Esau. Most scholars today are wary about precise dating or identification of the author of this book. A case has been made for several documentary theories, and dates have been assigned that range from 2000 to 200 B.C.

The Book of Job is the first example of "wisdom literature"

to occur in the Bible. There will be more in the Psalms, and the books of Proverbs and Ecclesiastes. Wisdom, in the Bible, invariably begins with the fear of the Lord, and is that quality of mind that enables a man to be successful himself and to counsel others well. Beyond that, it is depicted as a female personality who declares of herself that she was pre-existent with God (Prov. 8:22–31)—totally above, beyond, and apart from men who need to learn to love and cherish her, for, as she says, "All who hate me love death" (Prov. 8:36).

Of all the wisdom literature, the Book of Job is unequaled in its scope and profundity, moving with lyrical grace and majesty, as it explores themes that few authors would even dare to attempt. The narrative is filled with drama and pathos, probing to the depths of one man's soul. In or out of the Bible, it is a monumental epic.

GOD ALLOWS SATAN TO TEST JOB
JOB'S COMFORTERS
(Job 1–6, 8–9, 11)

1. Why did God allow Satan to test Job?
2. What does Job say about the day he was born? Why? Quote a typical statement in the chapter. Have you ever felt this way? When?
3. What does Eliphaz imply about Job's morality? Give textual evidence to back up your answer.
4. Give evidence showing that Job either admits or denies that he has sinned (chap. 6).
5. How does Bildad feel about Job's morality? Give textual evidence to support your answer.
6. What does Job say about his guilt or innocence in chapter 9?
7. How does Job's third comforter, Zophar, feel about Job's guilt or innocence (chap. 11)?
8. Review the attitudes of Job's three comforters. How much real comfort did they afford Job? What does the term

"Job's Comforter" mean, in view of the account you just read?

Job's Comforter: The phrase "Job's Comforter" today means someone who comes to a person in a time of grief, only to make that person feel worse than before.

JOB CONVERSES WITH GOD
JOB LEARNS A LESSON,
AND IS TWICE BLESSED
(Job 13, 38, 42)

1. In 13:23–24, Job asks God to tell him of what sin he is guilty. What is Job's guilt?
2. What point is Job making (through his list of examples in chapter 31) about his own morality?
3. What point does God make when he asks Job, "Where wast thou when I laid the foundations of the earth . . . and who hath laid the measures thereof" (38:4–5)?
4. In 42:1–6, Job shows that he has really learned the lesson God intended for him to learn. What lesson did he learn?
5. How does God show Job that he is pleased with the results of the "test" Job went through?

The Purpose of Testing: Why do the righteous suffer? The Bible teaches throughout that righteousness and wickedness will receive their due rewards—that the righteous man who meditates day and night in the law of God will prosper, while the wicked will be driven like chaff before the wind (Ps. 1). But in Job, a righteous man is deprived of everything but his life. His comforters conclude that this means Job is guilty of some sin, and set themselves to get him to confess, which Job resolutely refuses to do. In the last chapter, Job repents in the face of God's direct words to him, but God rebukes the comforters for their false accusations, which raises the question: Of what did Job repent?

Some would answer that chapter 42 was added much later by someone who wanted to solve the enigma and make Job repent in spite of his innocence; others simply throw up their hands, declaring the enigma unsolvable, arguing that the teaching of the book is that there is finally no explanation for the suffering of the righteous. A few have pointed to an intriguing possibility in God's speech in chapters 40 and 41 where two primeval creatures, Behemoth and Leviathan, are discussed at some length. Behemoth resembles a hippopotamus, immovable before even the rushing torrent of the Jordan. Leviathan emerges from the depths of the sea, a lurking serpentine monster who defies capture. Through these images, God, say the proponents of this view, is speaking of the mysterious nature of his deep work in the lives of his faithful servants, like Job. Behemoth represents self-will and Leviathan self-love, both of which are deeply seated in the human personality and can be retained intact in even the most righteous and pure life. When Job despises himself and repents in dust and ashes, it is because he sees that through his sufferings God seeks to reveal and remove these hidden monsters from his life.

THE PSALMS

It has been said that every nuance of human emotion is voiced somewhere in this collection of one hundred and fifty songs and poems. And indeed it is here that the intensely personal aspects of biblical religion are expressed, revealing the soul of this ancient people. The Psalms express varying degrees of adoration, confession, thanksgiving, or supplication as they utter the maxims of wisdom, recite the history of Israel's redemption, laud the king, or celebrate the faithfulness of God.

The Psalms are divided into five groups or books: 1–41, 42–72, 73–89, 90–106, 107–150. Nearly half of these songs are ascribed to David, who stood out as the foremost singer of

Israel (II Sam. 23:1). The sons of Korah, Jeduthun, Asaph, Heman, and Ethan are also mentioned as authors, while many of the psalms contain no information about authorship. The word *selah* occurs from time to time in the text of many psalms, and although no one really knows what it meant, it may have been a direction for an instrumental interlude without singing.

EXAMINING THE PSALMS
(Ps. 1, 5, 7–8, 14, 16, 21–23, 46, 51, 68–69,
103, 119, 124, 126–27, 137, 150)

1. Psalm 1: List the ways the author contrasts the righteous and the wicked.
2. Psalm 5: Apply this psalm to an event in David's life.
3. Psalm 8: With what aspect of God is the Psalmist most impressed?
4. Psalm 14: What is the author's definition of a fool?
5. Psalm 23: Why is this psalm appropriate for funerals? What other occasions would it fit?
6. Read Psalms 7, 21, 22, 16, 68, and 69. Argue a case for and against each psalm being "messianic." ("Messianic" means "prophetic of Jesus Christ," from a Christian point of view.)
7. Psalm 46: What is the most important attribute of God according to the Psalmist?
8. Psalm 51: Why is this called a penitential psalm?
9. Psalm 103: What quality of God is emphasized in this psalm?
10. Psalm 119: How does this psalm differ from all the other psalms you have read thus far?
11. Psalms 124 and 126: How are these psalms expressive of Jewish feeling concerning their history?
12. Psalm 127: According to this psalm, how can one have a guarantee of safety and success?
13. Psalm 137: Who is the speaker in this psalm?
14. Psalm 150: What are some ways in which one can praise God, according to the Psalmist?

Acrostic: Psalm 119 is an alphabetic acrostic. The first word of each section begins with a letter of the Hebrew alphabet from "A to Z." This arrangement produces a random collection of thoughts rather than a progression.

PROVERBS

The book of Proverbs is the central example of wisdom literature in the Bible, consisting primarily of pithy sayings about how to live wisely and avoid the way of the fool. Its four distinct sections (1–9; 10–22:16; 22:17–24; 25–29) are followed by a miscellaneous epilogue most famous for its portrait of the ideal wife (31:10–31).

Solomon, the traditional author of this book, was the king most noted for his wisdom (I Kings 3), and scholars agree that much of the content of Proverbs dates back to his day, arguing nevertheless that final compilation came at a later date. For an interesting discussion of authorship, consult the appropriate works listed under Tenney and Buttrick in the bibliography.

The typical poetical form for a Proverb is the couplet. There are three types.

1. Synonymous—The first line is extended in the second line. (Different words are used to restate the point made in the first line, as in 3:11.)
2. Antithetic—The second line contrasts with the first line, as in 14:34.
3. Synthetic—The second line concludes the first line. An example of this is 3:7.

THE TEACHING OF PROVERBS
(Selected Proverbs)

1. What is the purpose of the book of Proverbs, according to 1:1–6?

2. What is wisdom, according to 1:7? Explain how this works in life.

3. According to 1:20–33, what is the result of ignoring the principles of wisdom, and what is the result of following them?

4. What biblical principle is stated in 3:5–6?

5. What sin is the author warning against in chapter 5? Apply this to Solomon's life.

6. If you agreed with 11:4, what would your goal in life be?

7. Give an example to illustrate 11:2.

8. Read and summarize the following Proverbs: 6:6–11; 10:4; 12:27; 20:4; 20:13; 21:25; 22:13; 24:30–34; 26:13–16.

9. What important lesson do the following Proverbs teach about using words: 13:3; 15:1; 17:28; 19:11?

10. For each of the following Proverbs, state the form of foolish behavior against which the author is issuing a warning: 14:12; 15:8; 17:10; 22:3; 23:4–5; 23:29–35; 25:17; 26:7; 26:11; 26:27.

11. What lessons can we learn from the animals mentioned in 30:24–29?

12. What qualities define a virtuous woman (31:10–31)?

ECCLESIASTES

The third and final example of wisdom literature in the Bible, Ecclesiastes, expresses a philosopher's reflections on life "under the sun" (apart from God) with all its transient meaninglessness. Life is basically vain when considered in this framework, compelling men to enjoy whatever good is possible and to accept what cannot be changed. The inclusion of Ecclesiastes in the canon has often puzzled Bible readers, because its theme is so at variance with the dominant motifs of Scripture. The final verses (12:9–14) offer at least a partial solution, by stipulating the position from which the rest of the book is to be understood.

The first verse proclaims, "The words of the Preacher, the son of David, king in Jerusalem," pointing to Solomon, the traditional author. The word "preacher" is *Koheleth* in Hebrew from the stem *kahal* which means "assembly." *Ekklesia* is Greek for "assembly," hence the title.

Ernest Hemingway's famous novel, *The Sun Also Rises,* takes its title from Ecclesiastes 1:5.

THE MEANING OF LIFE
(Eccles. 1–3, 6, 9, 11–12)

1. By reading chapter 1, tell how the author feels about life.
2. Do you agree or disagree with 1:18? Why?
3. List some of the attempts made by the author to find happiness in life. What is the result of his attempts?
4. The author worries about something in 2:14–17. What is it?
5. Answer the problem posed in 3:16–22 in terms of what you have learned from previous readings. Apply a biblical principle in your answer.
6. What disturbs the speaker in 6:1–8? What is missing in his philosophy?
7. Ecclesiastes 9:11–12 is not consistent with a particular biblical principle. Which principle is this?
8. Explain the meaning of 11:1. Relate it to a biblical principle.
9. Read 11:1–6. How has the author begun to think positively? Quote something to back up your answer.
10. What is the main point of chapter 12? Why is this the most important chapter in the book? What effect would it have upon the book if chapter 12 were left out?
11. According to Ecclesiastes, what is man's purpose in life?

Imagery of Chapter 12: Chapter 12 is highly poetic. Verses 2–7 speak of an aged person who is rapidly losing physical capacity. The sun, light, moon, and stars represent the eyes dimming. The keepers of the house are the arms, and the strong men are the legs. The grinders are the teeth. The doors shut in the streets are lips, tightly closed with age. The sound of grinding will be low because the teeth are gone, and one can no longer chew. An old person frightens easily (rises up at the sound of a bird). The almond tree represents old age. The golden bowl suspended by a silver cord was a symbol of life. The breaking of the bowl was a symbol of death.

THE SONG OF SOLOMON
(Also called Song of Songs and Canticles)

The Song of Solomon is a love poem, a dialogue between two lovers, a man and his bride. Christians and Jews believe that it can be seen as symbolic of the relationship between God and his people. (Christians take it a step further, and see the book as a relationship between Christ and the Church, his bride.)

WAYS TO VIEW THE SONG OF SOLOMON
(Song of Sol. 1–8)

1. There are three characters (speakers) throughout most of the book. See if you can identify them in chapter 1. Which lines belong to the bride? Which belong to the groom? Which belong to the daughters of Jerusalem? (Consult an annotated Bible if you need help.)
2. How does the bride feel about losing her groom (chap. 3)? How does man feel when he cannot reach God? Which reading is most comfortable for you?
3. In chapters 4 and 7, the bride is described. If the bride is God's people, how does God feel about his people? How does Christ feel about his Church? How should a husband feel about his wife?
4. Chapter 7 describes the union of the bride and groom.

What feelings are expressed here? How does man feel when he is united with God? When will the Church be united with Christ? How is man united to woman in marriage?

5. What desire does the bride express in 8:6? If the bride represents God's people, what is the desire? If the bride represents the Church, what is the desire? If the bride represents a wife, what is her desire?

6. Which view is most comfortable for you, the love poem between a man and his bride, the relationship between God and his people, the relationship between Christ and the Church, or the teaching that marriage-love is God-ordained? Why is this view most comfortable for you? Which view do you think the author had in mind? Back up your argument with reasons.

The Prophetic Books

The final section of the Old Testament contains the works of the prophets of Israel. The books of the four major prophets (Isaiah, Jeremiah, Ezekiel, and Daniel) are followed by those of the twelve minor prophets (Hosea, Joel, Amos, Obadiah, Jonah, Micah, Nahum, Habakkuk, Zephaniah, Haggai, Zechariah, Malachi).

Because Israel's religion claimed not to be founded in metaphysical speculation, superstition, or philosophical reasoning, but in a revelation of God through historical events, the ministry of the prophet was fundamental to that religion. The prophet's role was to interpret the events of his day in light of God's laws and ways, and to issue forth God's warnings and promises to the people whose lives comprised that history.

In the Hebrew canon, the historical books are known as the "former prophets" because their purpose was not simply to recount the events of the succeeding years of Israel's history out of academic interest, but to record the revelation of God in and through that history. Thus prophecy was the very lifeblood of Israel's experience from the earliest times until the close of the Old Testament era.

ISAIAH

Through the ages, no book of the Old Testament has so consistently captivated its readers as has that of the eighth century (B.C.) prophet Isaiah. It is by far the most quoted book in the pages of the New Testament, reflecting the deep messianic strains that characterize the entire volume. Much of Handel's baroque masterpiece, *The Messiah,* is drawn verbatim from the Isaiah of the King James Version.

Isaiah is the first and the longest of the four major prophets of the Old Testament, characterized as "major" because their writings are more lengthy than those of the so-called minor prophets.

The eighth century B.C. was a great turning point in the history of Israel and Judah. Both kingdoms began the century in strength and prosperity, but by 700 B.C., Israel had fallen to the Assyrians, and Judah was seriously threatened, although it would be another 130 years before Jerusalem actually fell to a foreign aggressor, Babylonia. Isaiah's ministry began in 740 and concluded, according to ancient tradition, by his being sawed in pieces during the reign of Manasseh in 687. The peak of his career was reached in 701, when Jerusalem was surrounded by the armies of Sennacherib, king of Assyria. Basically helpless in the face of this crisis, Hezekiah, then king of Judah, cried out to God, and Isaiah prophesied that the city would stand, whereupon 185,000 men of the Assyrian army were mysteriously slain in the night by the angel of the Lord and Sennacherib was compelled to withdraw (II Kings 19; Isa. 36–37).

Isaiah is, of course, the traditional author of his own book, but in the last two centuries, many scholars have asserted that he was personally responsible for only chapters 1–39 and that the rest of the book was written much later in the sixth century—because chapters 40–66 contain references to Babylonia that even mention its king, Cyrus, by name. One school asserts that Isaiah wrote these chapters in his later life as predictive prophecy of events that were to develop about one hundred years after his own death. The opposing school claims that since such prediction is essentially unbelievable, we must conclude that the chapters were written by another person, one who was living during the time of Babylonian expansion.

These arguments, while interesting, primarily reflect their proponents' presuppositions about what is and what is not believable. They are not, however, essential for the appreciation of the book of Isaiah as the exquisite piece of literature it is, churning with moral earnestness and anguish for a people so unclean before their God and so deserving of his judgment, and yet presenting a God who promises to deliver his people by his coming Messiah, the conquering hero—a suffering servant.

PUNISHMENTS FOR THE NATIONS
ISAIAH'S VISION
APOCALYPSE
(Isa. 1–5, 6, 13–27)

1. List some of the sins mentioned in chapters 1–5. What will God do if the people repent? What will happen if they do not?
2. Describe Isaiah's vision of chapter 6. What effect does the vision have upon Isaiah's view of himself and God? What is Isaiah's commission?
3. Skim through chapters 13–23. List the nations prophesied against in those chapters.
4. Chapters 24–27 are called "The Isaiah Apocalypse." What is an apocalypse, and what elements in these chapters qualify them to be called apocalyptic?

PROPHECY OF ISRAEL
CHRIST
THE END OF THE WORLD
(Isa. 35, 42, 49–50, 53, 58, 62, 65–66)

1. When Israel became a nation in 1947, many Jews quoted 35:1 as having been fulfilled, especially when they began to irrigate the land. Do you agree or disagree with this interpretation? Justify your answer.

2. Argue a case for or against chapter 42 being a reference to Jesus Christ. Refer to the text.
3. According to 49:8–26, what will God ultimately do for Israel?
4. Argue a case for or against chapters 50 and 53 being prophetic of Jesus Christ as the Messiah.
5. According to chapter 58, what is true fasting?
6. What natural illustration is used to describe the relationship between God and his people in chapter 62?
7. According to 65:17–25, what will the new world be like? Has it arrived yet? Justify your answer.
8. What is being described in 66:22–24? Justify your answer.

JEREMIAH

Jeremiah has been called "the weeping prophet," because his was the grievous task of prophesying against Judah in the final days of that kingdom before its destruction at the hands of Nebuchadnezzar in 587 B.C. He had begun to preach in 627, during the reign of Josiah, whose reign had initiated some significant reforms, but throughout most of his career, Jeremiah was confronted by wholesale abandonment of the worship of the Lord (Yahweh) by both king and people. In the face of this apostasy, Jeremiah prophesied the destruction of Jerusalem, and in so doing, stood almost alone, for most of the other prophets were optimistically proclaiming peace and security for the holy city. His outspoken dissent from the prevailing opinion won him the scorn of his fellow prophets, whom he scorned in return, and even brought him to a severe imprisonment at the miry bottom of a well.

The book itself is a puzzle in its arrangement: it is obviously not chronological, and many theories have been advanced to explain the arrangement of the materials as we have them today. This matter and the other disputes about authorship and editorial emendations may be examined more closely by consulting books listed in the bibliography.

THE LIFE AND MINISTRY OF JEREMIAH
(Jer. 1–3, 7, 9, 18, 23, 26–28, 37)

1. God tells Jeremiah, "Before I formed thee in the belly I knew thee; and before thou camest forth out of the womb I sanctified thee, and I ordained thee a prophet unto the nations" (1:5). Explain the meaning of this statement, and relate it to a biblical principle.
2. What excuse does Jeremiah give God for not being able to prophesy, and what is God's answer?
3. Why is God disappointed with Israel (chap. 2)?
4. Why is an unfaithful wife an appropriate analogy for Israel (3:1–5)?
5. What does Jeremiah warn the people of in his "Temple Sermon" (7:13–14)?
6. God says that Israel is "uncircumcised in heart" (9:26). Explain the meaning of this statement.
7. Jeremiah, in 18:1–12, prophesies, using the analogy of a potter with a vessel. Explain the meaning of this analogy, relating it to God and his people.
8. Jeremiah 23:5–8 is considered by some to be messianic. Explain how this is so. Then give your own view on whether or not it is indeed messianic.
9. Why do the people try to kill Jeremiah?
10. What advice does Jeremiah give the people concerning Babylon? Contrast Jeremiah's advice with Hananiah's advice. (Read chaps. 26–28.)
11. What does the yoke symbolize?
12. What happens to Jeremiah in chapter 37?

God's Plan for One's Life: Jeremiah's name may mean "Yahweh appoints or establishes," denoting the emphasis on predestination in this book. God commissioned Jeremiah to announce that Judah's sins had provoked irrevocable judgment for her and that to prevent unnecessary bloodshed, she should capitulate to Babylon without resistance. Jeremiah endured the ferocious antagonism against him that his message aroused by the inward assurance that his God had appointed him for this task even before he had been born. God's sovereign control of history, and of the lives of men in it, has perennially perplexed and disturbed men of every walk of life, and yet it has afforded comfort and assurance for tens of thousands of people facing grim situations.

LAMENTATIONS

The Lamentations of Jeremiah are a series of elegies lamenting the fate of Jerusalem, after it was besieged and destroyed by the Babylonians in 587 B.C. The book consists of five chapters, each of which is an alphabetic acrostic in the original Hebrew.

Some scholars believe that someone other than Jeremiah, perhaps a committee, wrote the book. For a discussion of this, see the works by Tenney and Buttrick listed in the bibliography.

THE LAMENTATIONS OF JEREMIAH
(Lam. 1–5)

1. Jerusalem is said to be like a "widow" (1:1). Why is this an appropriate analogy?
2. Does the author deny or affirm the guilt of Jerusalem? Justify your answer by the text.
3. What are the people admonished to do in chapter 3?
4. What is Jeremiah's plea to God in chapter 5?
5. From what you already know about the biblical God, do you think God will answer Jeremiah's plea? When and under what conditions? Justify your answer by referring to various parts of the Bible.

EZEKIEL

Ezekiel prophesied as a captive in Babylon where he had been deported in 597 B.C., about ten years before the final overthrow of Jerusalem and the destruction of the Temple. His ministry extended until 571 B.C. and was directed to his fellow exiles, to Jerusalem and its inhabitants, and to the foreign nations of Ammon, Tyre, Philistia, and Egypt. After the fall of Jerusalem, he spoke to reassure his fellow exiles of God's continuing presence and activity among them. The events of those days, he asserted, were ordained by the Lord so that Israel and the nations might "know that I am the Lord" (a frequently recurring refrain in the book). Emphasizing the personal responsibility of each man to God, he foresaw a future restoration of the homeland and Temple at the hands of a just and holy God.

Ezekiel's book, unlike that of his contemporary Jeremiah, is very orderly and clear in its arrangement. Its three divisions treat three principal subjects: (1) warnings of the impending disaster in Jerusalem (1–24); (2) oracles against the nations (25–32); (3) promises of the future restoration of Israel (33–48).

THE MINISTRY OF EZEKIEL
(Ezek. 1–3, 16, 18, 24, 26, 37, 40–42)

1. Describe Ezekiel's vision. Try to explain the symbolism. What is your impression of God after reading this account (chap. 1)?
2. To whom was Ezekiel called? Why was this a difficult calling (chap. 2)?
3. Explain the symbolism of the book written "within and without" (2:9–10).
4. In Ezekiel 3:1, God tells Ezekiel to eat the scroll. Explain the symbolism of this act.
5. Explain the allegory demonstrating Israel's apostasy (chap. 16).

6. What promise does God renew at the end of chapter 16?
7. Describe the principle of individual responsibility (chap. 18).
8. What was the meaning of the death of Ezekiel's wife (chap. 24)?
9. What did Ezekiel prophesy would happen to Tyre (chap. 26)?
10. What do the dry bones of chapter 37 symbolize?
11. Explain 37:21–28 in terms of your own thinking. Many scholars see a messianic prophecy here. What is their reasoning? (Indicate the texts that could be messianic prophecy.)
12. What is the topic of discussion in chapters 40–42? Why is that topic so important to the Jews? What might the Temple symbolize? Justify your answer by the text. Work out a system of symbolism to justify your answer.

Ezekiel's Vision: The bizarre elements of Ezekiel's vision require some research for understanding. How is one to understand the four living creatures and the wheels? And how do they convey an image of the glory of the Lord? Various interesting explanations of Ezekiel's vision are recorded in the *New Bible Commentary* (see bibliography).

The Scroll Written Within and Without: A scroll written within and without is meant to convey a sense of weightiness or importance to the message contained on the parchment. The words are so important that they literally burn through, etching both sides of the scroll.

The City-State of Tyre: The city-state of Tyre (chap. 26) was the ancient center of the worldwide Phoenician commercial empire. Located on an isle immediately adjacent to the shoreline of Lebanon, it was a virtually impregnable fortress until Alexander the Great overran it after a siege of seven months. Around thirty thousand of its inhabitants were sold into slavery, and two thousand of the leaders were hanged. Today,

Tyre, renamed Sur, is a small fishing village of about six thousand people.

DANIEL

No book of the Old Testament has been embroiled in more controversy than the Book of Daniel; as early as the third century of the Christian era, Porphyry, a Neoplatonist philosopher, argued that the book was a forgery written in the Maccabean period (*ca.* 165 B.C.) to encourage Jews to be faithful in the face of the persecutions of Antiochus Epiphanes. The interested student is referred to the bibliography for further study.

In the text, Daniel is just a lad when he is deported to Babylon after the fall of Jerusalem in 587 B.C. From there, we get glimpses of his life into old age, as he passes through increasingly severe tests of his faith in company with his three associates, Shadrach, Meshach, and Abednego. The book is filled with apocalyptic imagery—it is, in fact, the supreme Old Testament specimen of apocalyptic literature. Whatever the opinions of its historicity, this book has perennially delighted and intrigued youngsters and oldsters alike with its wicked Babylonians, haunting visions, and miraculous escapes, all bound together in a sense of holy mystery.

THE FAITHFULNESS OF DANIEL
THE KING'S DREAM
THE FIERY FURNACE
(Dan. 1–4)

1. Why wouldn't Daniel eat the king's food? What does this tell you about his morality?
2. Describe the king's dream, and tell what Daniel's interpretation was.
3. Why were Shadrach, Meshach, and Abednego put into the furnace?

THE WRITING ON THE WALL
THE LION'S DEN
A REVELATION OF THE FUTURE
(Dan. 5–12)

1. What evil thing did Belshazzar do at his feast?
2. What was the meaning of the message written on the wall? What was Daniel's reward for interpreting it?
3. How did the princes get Daniel put into the lions' den? How did the king feel about this?
4. What effect did Daniel's miraculous escape from death in the lions' den have upon the king?
5. After reading chapter 12 carefully, tell to what time period it refers. Justify your answer carefully, using the text.

HOSEA

Hosea is always remembered as the prophet with the unfaithful wife. His predicament, into which he was directed by the Lord, was to be a living illustration of the Lord's relationship with unfaithful Israel. His excruciating humiliation and the poignant tenderness of his life with Gomer was his oracle to the apostate northern kingdom shortly before it fell to the Assyrians in 722 B.C.

HOSEA'S MARRIAGE
A CALL TO REPENTANCE
(Hos. 1–4, 7–9, 11, 13–14)

1. What was wrong with Hosea's marriage? How did his marital problem relate to his prophecy to Israel?
2. Of what sin were the priests guilty (chap. 4)?
3. What result did the inner depravity of Israel have upon the nation (chap. 7)?

4. What would happen if Israel continued to sin (chaps. 8–9)?
5. How did God feel about Israel, even though she was sinful (chap. 11)?
6. What did God ask for in 13:9–14, and chapter 14?

JOEL

The book of Joel was written when a natural catastrophe had occurred in the land of Israel, a plague of locusts. Joel makes a comparison between the invasion of the locusts and the Day of the Lord. The horror of the coming Day of the Lord is emphasized by the intensity of the plague, which brought destruction and death.

Of Joel himself, nothing is known, and only conjecture can be made about the date or immediate background of his book.

JOEL SPEAKS OF THE DAY OF THE LORD
THE HOLY SPIRIT AND THE RENEWED PROMISE
(Joel 1–3)

1. What natural catastrophe occurs in the land?
2. What is Joel's remedy for the catastrophe?
3. What is the Day of the Lord, and when will it come? Justify your answer by the text (chap. 2).
4. Joel 2:28–32 talks about a revival in which God will pour out his Spirit, and young and old alike will experience a spiritual awakening. Argue a case for: 1) The prophecy is being fulfilled now; or, 2) The prophecy has already been fulfilled. Use the text. Then give your own view.
5. Explain the meaning of 3:1–8. When does it take place? Justify your answer by using the text.
6. What will happen after the sinful nations are judged (chap. 3)?

7. What promise is given to the Jews as Joel concludes his prophecy?

Joel's "Latter Day" Prophecy: One of the more lengthy single quotes of an Old Testament passage in the New Testament is recorded in Peter's proclamation on the day of Pentecost (Acts 2) when he cited Joel 2:28–32 to explain the strange phenomenon of glossolalia (speaking in tongues) so much in evidence that momentous morning. Glossolalia has emerged once more in the twentieth century, fomenting new controversy in the religious community as evidenced by the proliferation of books on the subject, *e.g., They Speak with Other Tongues* by John Sherrill, *Speaking in Tongues* by Laurence Christenson, and *What about Tongue-Speaking?* by Anthony Hoekema.

AMOS

The long and peaceful reign of Jeroboam II (786–746 B.C.) marked the period of the northern kingdom's greatest prosperity and territorial expansion, which were signs, in the minds of many Israelites, of the Lord's favor toward their country. Amos had the difficult task of pronouncing God's doom upon this contented people—he dubbed them "cows of Bashan" (4:1)—who, despite their lavish support of official shrines (which they thought pleased God), were guilty of flagrant Baal worship, cultic prostitution, and even human sacrifice. Yet Amos, in the face of bitter opposition, approached his job with a ferocious zeal that established him as one of the most severe prophets of all time.

Amos was a Judean, a shepherd from the village of Tekoa, and had to travel out of his own territory northward in order to perform his ministry. His ministry was so unpopular that he was expelled from the shrine at Bethel (7:12) and had to return to Judah. It was probably there that he compiled his book.

THE PROPHECY OF AMOS
(Amos 1–3, 5, 7–9)

1. Which nations are denounced in chapters 1–2? Are these mythological or actual nations?
2. Why will God punish Israel (chap. 3)?
3. What three woes are prophesied in chapter 3?
4. What does the vision of fire symbolize?
5. What does the vision of the fruitbasket symbolize?
6. Read 9:8–10. Will all of Israel be destroyed? If not, who will be saved?
7. Read 9:11–15. When does this take place? Justify your answer.

Prophecy Concerning the Land of Israel: Many Jewish scholars (and a number of non-Jewish scholars as well) interpret Amos 9:15 as prophetic of the events in Palestine in 1947. (Read the novel *Exodus,* by Leon Uris, for a captivating story dealing with this theme.)

OBADIAH

Obadiah, a tiny book, the shortest of the Old Testament, has one theme—the Lord's anger against Edom, a kingdom southeast of Palestine at the southern tip of the Dead Sea. Of Obadiah, nothing is known except that this book is attributed to him.

The Edomites traced their origin, according to the Bible, back to Esau, the man who, though he was the elder son of Isaac, lost his birthright to his brother Jacob (Gen. 25:19–34; 27:1–41). Their personal hostility is understood to be the source of the national hostility between Edom and the house of Jacob.

OBADIAH'S WARNING TO EDOM
(Obad. 1)

1. Explain verse 10: "For thy violence against thy brother Jacob shame shall cover thee and thou shalt be cut off for ever."
2. Explain verses 17–21. What period of time is being discussed here? Justify your answer by using the text.

JONAH

If Daniel sparked more controversy than any other book of the Bible among scholars, then Jonah's book takes top honors for engendering disputes among laymen. Through the ages, this human story of a man who ran away when God spoke to him has enchanted its readers. But when it comes to his surviving three days and nights in the belly of a whale (the text says simply "fish," but folklore has identified it more particularly, just as it dubbed the forbidden fruit an apple)—and not just any whale, mind you, but a whale ordained by God to escort the wayward prophet back to his original assignment, well, that's just too much to be believed for many. They relegate it to the category of parable, myth, and legend, and interpret it accordingly.

Those of a more credulous frame of mind point to the mention of a prophet named Jonah from Gath-hepher near the sea of Galilee who counseled Jeroboam II (786–746 B.C.). He, they say, was identical to the Jonah of maritime fame, and few scholars would argue that there is not some direct connection, if not identity, between them. Furthermore, Jesus himself recalled the submarine journey of Jonah (Matt. 12:40), a fact which satisfies many as to the veracity of this famous tale.

Unlike any other of the books of the minor prophets, Jonah is nonetheless genuinely prophetic in that its narrative effectively summons Israel to return to her task of proclaiming to all nations that there is a just God in heaven who is rich in mercy, delighting to forgive the sin of those who repent.

JONAH, THE RELUCTANT MISSIONARY
(Jon. 1–4)

1. Why was Jonah cast into the sea and swallowed by the whale?
2. What change takes place in Jonah while he is in the fish (chap. 2)?
3. Why didn't God keep his word and destroy Nineveh?
4. Why was Jonah angry when God didn't destroy Nineveh?
5. What lesson did God teach Jonah by creating and then destroying the gourd?
6. What is the main point, moral, or theme of the book?
7. What is your interpretation of the book – history, allegory, parable, or legend? Give your reasons.
8. List three miraculous elements in the book and argue either for or against the possibility of their historicity.

Can a Man be Swallowed by a Whale and Live? A whale hunter, James Bartley, was swallowed by a whale in 1891. A day later, the whale was cut open, and James Bartley was still alive, although it was a month before he was able to think clearly.

Micah

Micah was a contemporary of Isaiah and shared that great prophet's earnest zeal for true worship and public and private righteousness. Unlike the urban Isaiah (a resident of Jerusalem), Micah lived in the little village of Moresheth in the Judean foothills southwest of Jerusalem. His small-town perspective made the pretensions of the big city seem less impressive, so that he even prophesied the fall of Jerusalem, a thing which none of his contemporaries, including Isaiah, dared to do (cf. Jer. 26:18).

The burden of this plucky prophet's message was directed against Samaria, the capital of the northern kingdom. His ministry extended from before 735 until after 715 and was probably much longer than twenty years. Samaria fell to the Assyrians, who deported its inhabitants, in 722.

Amos, who flourished earlier in the eighth century, came from Tekoa, which lay less than twenty miles from Micah's home. No doubt as Micah grew to manhood, he became familiar with Amos' cry for justice and owed much to him for the content of his own preaching.

THE PROPHECY OF MICAH
(Mic. 1–7)

1. What is Samaria's most offensive sin? Why is this sin particularly offensive to God?
2. What is Judah's main offense in chapter 2?
3. In chapter 4, Micah describes the "New Israel." When is he expecting this to happen? Justify your answer by using the text.
4. What will happen to Judah because of her corrupt leaders (see chap. 3)?
5. Micah 5:2–4 is held by many to be a messianic prophecy. Do you agree or disagree? Argue your case using the text.
6. Read 6:6–8. What pleases God more than ritual sacrifice? Why?
7. What characteristic of God is emphasized in Micah 7:18–20?

NAHUM

One of the most earth-shaking events of ancient history in the Near East was the dramatic overthrow of the proud Assyrian empire, for centuries the rulers of that vast crescent between Mesopotamia and the Mediterranean. The hallmark of Assyrian supremacy had been their barbaric treatment of their enemies; ancient art depicts Assyrian atrocities perhaps unrivaled elsewhere in history.

After the death of Ashurbanipal (*ca.* 630 B.C.), the empire began to rapidly deteriorate under the combined assaults of the Medes and Chaldeans. Ashur fell in 614 B.C. Two years later, the empire expired completely when its greatest city, the immense Nineveh, also collapsed before Medo-Babylonian onslaught.

Nahum's prophecies were directed entirely against Nineveh, attributing its downfall to the righteous indignation of the Lord against a proud and wicked nation. Little is known of Nahum himself. Elkosh, his hometown, may have been a village in Galilee.

NAHUM'S PROPHECY AGAINST ASSYRIA
(Nah. 1-3)

1. What is Nahum's overall impression of his God in chapter 1?
2. According to chapters 2 and 3, what will happen to Nineveh, the capital of Assyria?
3. From a biblical point of view, was Nahum justified in his delight with the pending destruction of his enemies?

HABAKKUK

Many scholars agree that Habakkuk was written between 605 and 587 B.C. This was just before Judah was completely captured, a time when political corruption and idolatry were rampant. The book itself is a theodicy, an explanation of the existence of evil.

HABAKKUK'S CONVERSATION WITH GOD
(Hab. 1-3)

1. What is Habakkuk's complaint to God in chapters 1 and 2, and what is God's answer?
2. What attribute of God does Habakkuk extol in chapter 3, and why does he extol this particular attribute?

ZEPHANIAH

Zephaniah prophesied during the reign of Josiah, approximately 640–609 B.C. This was just before Jeremiah, who may have been influenced by Zephaniah.

Zephaniah's main theme is coming judgment, the Day of the Lord. He protests the worshiping of idols and other religious depravities. His prophecy ends on the positive note of a coming restoration of Zion and the saving of the Jews.

THE PROPHECY OF ZEPHANIAH
(Zeph. 1–3)

1. What sin does Zephaniah decry in chapter 1?
2. Whom does God (through the prophecy of Zephaniah) warn of coming judgment in chapter 2?
3. What are the characteristics of the remnant described in chapter 3?
4. What period of time is being described in 3:14–20? Justify your answer by using the text.

Is the Prophecy of Zephaniah Already Fulfilled? Many religious Jews believe that Zephaniah 3:14–20 is a prophecy already fulfilled. They believe that God has brought them to their homeland, and has "gathered them that are sorrowful" (v. 18). They also believe that he will "undo all that afflict" Israel (v. 19). They also believe that God will "make you a name and a praise among all people of the earth" (v. 20). (See the appendix article, "Modern Israel," pp. 153–157.)

HAGGAI

Haggai prophesied after the exile, during the time when the Temple was being rebuilt, approximately 520 B.C. The thrust of his prophecy is to encourage the Jews to rebuild the Temple, in spite of the many obstacles facing them. His function was to help them to overcome a defeatist spirit, which was brought on by the Samaritan hindrances. (Work had been stopped because of the Samaritans, until Darius ascended the throne.) Haggai spoke five prophetic oracles.

HAGGAI ENCOURAGES THE REBUILDING OF THE TEMPLE (Hag. 1–2)

1. What does Haggai ask the people to do, and why does he insist that they do it?
2. What particular encouragement does God give the people (through Haggai) about the second Temple?
3. What does God promise the people if they rebuild the Temple?
4. In 2:23, Haggai says that God will make Zerubabel a signet. What does this mean?

ZECHARIAH

Zechariah spoke in the same year as Haggai, shortly after he did. His mission, also, was to encourage the Jews to continue rebuilding the Temple until the job was completed. According to traditional scholars, he wrote the book close to 520 B.C. Some scholars, however, believe that chapters 9–14 were written at a later date. The book is apocalyptic at times in that it speaks of the coming of the Messiah.

THE PROPHECY OF ZECHARIAH
(Zech. 1–6, 8–9, 12)

1. Chapters 1–6 describe eight symbolic visions, each one having the same message. What is it?
2. What period of time is being discussed in chapter 8? Justify your answer by referring to the text.

3. To whom does 9:9–10 refer? Justify your answer by using the text.
4. To whom does 12:10 refer? Justify your answer by using the text.

The Christian View of Zechariah's Prophecy: Christians believe that Zechariah delivered a messianic prophecy that was fulfilled by Jesus. They believe that 9:9 refers to his coming into Jerusalem on Palm Sunday (John 12:14–15), riding upon the foal of an ass, and they see in 12:10 a prophetic depiction of the piercing of Jesus' side by the soldier (John 19:34–37).

Dr. H. J. Schonfield, author of *The Passover Plot,* claims that Jesus realized that the Messiah was supposed to come into Jerusalem on a donkey, so he made sure that he did this.

MALACHI

In the last book of the minor prophets, we are confronted by the strong preaching of a prophet who lived in the first half of the fifth century B.C. (500–450). Nothing is known of the man's background or identity; his name means "my messenger" and may be an appellation based on the words of 3:1, "Behold, I send my messenger to prepare the way before me" (RSV).

Couched in an intriguing question-and-answer style, Malachi's message stresses faithfulness to the covenant between Israel and the Lord. He indicts the priests for corrupting true worship and misleading the people. In all, his book is a moving call to repentance and reform.

THE PROPHECY OF MALACHI
(Mal. 1–4)

1. Of what sins are the priests guilty (chap. 1)?
2. Explain the meaning of 1:11: "My name shall be great among the Gentiles."

3. To whom does 3:1-4 refer? Justify your answer by using the text.
4. How were the people robbing God (3:8-12)?
5. What blessing is promised to those who tithe?
6. In 4:1, reference is made to the wicked burning like stubble. Is this literal or figurative?
7. To whom does 4:2 refer? Justify your answer by the text.
8. Malachi 4:5-6 tells of the coming of Elijah the prophet before the Day of the Lord. Does this mean that God is saying he will resurrect Elijah? If not, what is he saying?

Tithing: Tithing is an established biblical requirement. Malachi rebukes the priests and the people for neglecting to fulfill this requirement (3:8-12). The people were supposed to give ten percent of all their goods to the work of God. Tithing was as mandatory as the current federal income tax. From this biblical principle, many Christians and Jews today still give ten percent of their income to their churches and synagogues.

The Coming of Elijah: Because of the reference to Elijah's coming before the advent of the Messiah, Jews believe that either Elijah himself, or one with a similar ministry, will appear before the Messiah arrives. Christians, however, believe that John the Baptist was the one God sent in the spirit of Elijah (Matt. 17:10-13).

The New Testament

The Gospels

"Gospel" is a very old Anglo-Saxon (Early English) word spelled *godspell,* which originally meant *good spell, good story, good news* (thus translating the Greek, *euangelion,* good tidings). In popular English usage, by dropping the second "o" in good, it came to mean God's story. The Greek has come into our language more directly, producing the word "evangel" and its derivatives, "evangelist," "evangelistic," and "evangelical."

The Gospels tell the "gospel" of Jesus Christ, that is, the good news about his birth, baptism, ministry of healing and teaching, death and resurrection. They are not biography in the contemporary sense of that word and do not purport to be exhaustive reports of the life of Jesus. In fact the Gospels focus almost entirely, with the exception of the birth narratives, upon the final three years of his life following his baptism in the Jordan river by John the Baptist.

Three of the Gospel narratives (Matthew, Mark, and Luke) are remarkably similar, so much so that they are called the "Synoptic (look-alike) Gospels." Tradition and scholarship both affirm that these Synoptic Gospels were written before the Fourth Gospel (John). Jesus himself left no written records, and it appears now that the first attempt to reduce the story to writing was made by John Mark, who, according to tradition, was a disciple of the apostle Peter. Mark's Gospel was, in turn, used by Matthew and Luke, along with a collection of *logia* (sayings of Jesus) and some other data, as the basis for their Gospels. There are two reasons for this theory that Mark was a source for Matthew and Luke: (1) Almost every verse of Mark appears also, in identical form, in either Matthew or Luke; (2) In the actual sequence of narrative, Matthew and Luke never agree together against Mark; either one or the other always concurs with him.

The work of John stands in marked contrast to the Synoptics. The earlier Gospels are set largely in Galilee, while John describes Jesus' early Judean ministry. Parables, as they are familiar to us from Matthew, Mark, and Luke, do not occur in the Fourth Gospel, which is characterized by its extensive discourses dealing with the union of the Christian believer with Christ.

MATTHEW

The First Gospel is traditionally considered to have been written by Matthew, the tax-collector whom Jesus called to follow him (Matt. 9:9). It presents Jesus as the Messiah and Lord of God's people, fulfilling the will and promises of God throughout the Old Testament. The common symbol for Matthew's Gospel is the lion, depicting Christ as the mighty king in regal splendor.

The most notable features of the book are its five great discourses on particular themes: chapters 5–7, The Sermon on the Mount; chapter 10, Missionary Instructions; chapter 13, The Parables of the Kingdom of God; chapter 18, The Requirements of Discipleship; chapters 24–25, The End of the World (the Olivet Discourse).

The author nowhere identifies himself in the text, the superscription, "according to Matthew," having been added at a later date. Scholars date the Gospel variously between A.D. 60 and 90.

THE BIRTH OF CHRIST
JOHN THE BAPTIST
THE TEMPTATION OF CHRIST
(Matt. 1–4)

1. Why does Matthew trace the lineage of Jesus through Abraham, Judah, and David?
2. According to Matthew, what was miraculous about the birth of Christ? What was Joseph's reaction when he realized that his fiancée was expecting a baby?
3. How did Herod plan to destroy Jesus? Why did he want to do this? How did Jesus escape death?
4. What prophecy does Matthew show as being fulfilled when Mary and Joseph escape to Egypt?
5. Micah 5:2 says that the Messiah must come from Bethlehem. How does Matthew show that this has been fulfilled?
6. What was the message of John the Baptist?
7. What was the purpose of Jesus' being baptized?
8. What were the three attempts made by the devil to get Jesus to sin? What was Jesus' answer in each case? Each temptation represents a type of temptation common to human beings in general. What does each temptation represent?
9. Name the four disciples listed in 4:18–25.

Jesus Christ: The name Jesus means "the Lord will Save." "Christ" means "Anointed one."

Poinsettia: The poinsettia symbolizes the star which the wise men followed to the manger, where they found Christ. It is often used to decorate homes during the Christmas season.

Christmas Gifts: The custom of gift-giving at Christmas comes from the account of the wise men bringing gifts to the infant Jesus.

THE SERMON ON THE MOUNT
(Matt. 5–7)

1. Read the beatitudes listed in 5:1–12. Compare and contrast them to the ten commandments. How are they similar? How are they different?
2. In 5:13–16, Jesus calls his followers the "salt of the earth." What does salt symbolize? He also calls his followers the "light of the world." What does light symbolize?
3. In 5:17–20, Jesus says he did not come to destroy the law, but rather to fulfill the law. How is this so? Give an example.
4. Jesus extends the commandment, "Thou shalt not commit adultery." How does he do this?
5. In 5:31–32, Jesus gives one case where it is morally correct to get a divorce. What case is this?
6. What is Jesus' advice about revenge (5:38–48)?
7. Jesus says, "Be ye therefore perfect, even as your Father which is in heaven is perfect" (5:48). How can one do this?
8. In 6:1–6 and 6:16–18, Jesus talks about showing off one's goodness. Why does a person who does this displease God?
9. What are the legitimate concerns of man about which he should pray, according to Jesus' teaching in the Lord's Prayer (6:9–15)?
10. How should one feel about material possessions (6:19–34)? Why?
11. What is true of most people who judge others? Why?
12. What is the condition for an answer to prayer (7:7–11)?
13. Read 7:12. What familiar "rule" is this?
14. In 7:13–14, Jesus says that the gate leading to eternal life is narrow. How is this so?
15. Who will actually get to heaven, after all is said and done (7:15–23)?

MIRACLES OF CHRIST
ADVICE TO DISCIPLES
(Matt. 8-10)

1. List the miracles performed by Christ in chapters 8 and 9. Why did Christ perform each of these miracles? (Read carefully.)
2. Relate the parable of the wineskins and old garments to people who try to follow the teachings of Christ. Give an example of one who "sews new cloth unto an old garment."
3. To whom should the disciples preach the message? Whom should they avoid?
4. What point does Jesus make in 10:28-33?
5. In what sense did Jesus come to bring a sword rather than peace to the earth?
6. What did Jesus mean by "He that taketh not his cross and followeth after me is not worthy of me" (10:38)?

JESUS AND JOHN
THE PHARISEES AND THE SABBATH
PARABLES OF JESUS
(Matt. 11-13)

1. Jesus complains that the people are like children who are never satisfied with what God does (11:16-19). How do the people exhibit this in their reaction to Jesus and John?
2. What is Jesus' yoke, and why is it easy?
3. How does Jesus show that he is "Lord of the Sabbath" in chapter 12?
4. How does Jesus prove that he is not in league with the devil (12:22-28)?
5. Why could the unclean Spirit re-enter the man from whom he had been expelled (12:43-45)?

6. With whom is Jesus really pleased (12:46–50)?
7. What is the moral of the parable of the sower?
8. What do the parables of the weeds and the net (13:24–30; 13:47–52) teach about judgment day?
9. What do the parables of the mustard seed and leaven (13:31–33) teach about the kingdom of heaven?
10. What common moral do the parables of the treasure and the pearl have (13:44–46)?
11. Why did Jesus use parables in his teaching?

A House Divided: Lincoln used a portion of Matthew 12:25 in his famous "House Divided" speech before the Civil War.

JOHN AND HEROD
THE FEEDING OF THE FIVE THOUSAND
PETER IS CALLED SATAN
THE TRANSFIGURATION
(Matt. 14, 16–17)

1. Why was John beheaded?
2. Why did Jesus perform the miracle of the loaves and fishes in chapter 14?
3. What did Jesus mean when he called Peter, Satan (16:21–28)?
4. What was the purpose of the transfiguration (chap. 17)?

CHILDREN
THE UNMERCIFUL SERVANT
THE SEX DRIVE
ETERNAL LIFE
(Matt. 18–20)

1. In what sense must one become childlike in order to please God?
2. Peter asked Jesus how many times one must forgive a

person for an offense. Read the parable of 18:21–35. What is Jesus' answer?

3. Does Jesus acknowledge the "sex drive" (19:1–11)?

4. Why wouldn't the man in 19:16–30 follow Jesus? What lesson is to be learned from this?

5. What is the meaning of the parable of the householder (20:1–16)?

JESUS ENTERS JERUSALEM
THE PARABLE OF THE MARRIAGE FEAST
TEACHING ON THE RESURRECTION
(Matt. 21–23)

1. Zechariah 9:9 states that the prophesied Messiah will ride into the holy city upon the foal of an ass. Quote Matthew's claimed fulfillment of this prophecy.

2. Why did Jesus cast the money changers out of the Temple?

3. Jesus said, "If ye shall say unto this mountain, Be thou removed, and be thou cast into the sea; it shall be done" (21:21). What does he mean?

4. In 21:28–32, Jesus tells of two sons. Why did the "bad" one please his father in the end? Who are the bad, younger sons of Jesus' generation? Who are the bad, younger sons of your generation?

5. Explain the meaning of the parable of the householder and the vineyard (21:33–46).

6. Explain the parable of the marriage feast (22:1–14).

7. What did Jesus teach about obeying the law?

8. How is life in heaven different from life on earth (22:23–32)?

9. In 22:31–32, Jesus proves to the Sadducees that there is "eternal life." How does he do this?

10. What is Jesus' complaint against the Pharisees (chap. 23)?

THE END OF THE WORLD
(Matt. 24–25)

1. List the signs of the end times mentioned in chapter 24. Justify a case for either: "The end times are upon us now," or "These signs have always been with us." Use the text and your own arguments to defend your position.
2. What manifestations will Christ take when he appears?
3. Relate the parable of the fig tree to the coming of Christ (24:32–35).
4. How do the days of Noah compare to the end times?
5. How will the believers be taken to heaven?
6. What lesson is taught in 24:45–51?
7. What is the moral of the parable of the ten virgins (25:1–13)?
8. What is the moral of the parable of the talents (25:14–30)?
9. Read 25:31–46. Whom do the sheep and goats represent? What is the moral?

Talent: The talent was originally a measure of money. Later, it came to mean "God-given ability."

DEATH AND RESURRECTION
(Matt. 26–28)

1. Who wanted to kill Jesus? Why?
2. What evidence is there in chapter 26 that Jesus knew he was going to die?
3. What does Jesus mean when he tells his disciples to eat his body and drink his blood (26:26–29)?
4. What prophecy does Jesus make concerning Peter? Does it happen? When?
5. Give evidence that Jesus suffered before going to the cross.
6. Why did the priests ask for the release of Barabbas, a thief, rather than Jesus, a good man?

7. Why did Pilate wash his hands in front of all the people?
8. Why did Jesus ask God why he had forsaken him (27:46)? *Did* God forsake him?
9. What signs accompanied the death of Christ (27:45–53)?
10. Why did the Pharisees ask Pilate to guard the tomb (27:62–64)?
11. What did the scribes and Pharisees do when they heard that Jesus had actually arisen? Why did they do this?
12. What command did Jesus give his disciples before ascending into heaven?
13. What promise did Jesus give his disciples?

MARK

Ancient Christian tradition attributes the Second Gospel to John Mark (Acts 12:12; 15:37), who is supposed to have compiled it in Rome as a summary of the apostle Peter's preaching (cf. I Pet. 5:13). It is generally dated between A.D. 50 and 70, and is held to be the first Gospel written down.

In Mark, Jesus is the Son of God, performing mighty works which announce the coming of God's reign upon earth for those with ears to hear. The Greek word *euthus,* meaning "immediately," occurs over forty times in the book, a fact which points up the extent to which Jesus is depicted as almost constantly active. There are fewer sayings of Jesus here than in any other Gospel, and there is only one solid discourse (chap. 13). The common emblem for Mark the evangelist is an ox.

THE BEGINNINGS OF THE MINISTRY OF CHRIST
(Mark 1–3, 5)

1. How does Mark's account of the early life and ministry of Christ differ from Matthew's account?
2. What events mark the beginnings of Christ's ministry? Make a list.

3. Why were the scribes angry when Jesus healed the man with the palsy?
4. What was Jesus' reason for associating with low-class people and "sinners"?
5. Jesus says, "The sabbath was made for man, and not man for the sabbath" (2:27). What did he mean by this?

THE PHARISEES
FAITH
THE SOUL
(Mark 7–8)

1. In 7:1–13, the Pharisees miss the true meaning of the law. How?
2. Why did Jesus heal the Gentile woman's daughter after having first refused?
3. Jesus told his disciples, "Take heed, beware of the leaven of the Pharisees, and of the leaven of Herod." What did he mean by this?
4. What did people think of Jesus' ministry? Did they think he was the Messiah (chap. 8)?
5. Jesus says, "Whosoever will save his life shall lose it; but whosoever shall lose his life for my sake and the gospel's, the same shall save it" (8:35). Explain what he means by this statement.
6. In Mark 8:36–37, Jesus asks what it will profit a man if he gains the whole world but loses his soul. He also asks what a man can give in exchange for his soul. Answer these questions.

THE PARABLE OF THE VINEYARD
THE WIDOW'S MITE
THE RESURRECTION
(Mark 12, 16)

1. What was Jesus trying to teach the Pharisees when he said that David called the Christ Lord (12:36–37)?

2. What lesson did Jesus teach his disciples by the widow's offering?
3. What did the women find when they came to anoint Jesus after his death?
4. What did the angel tell the women?
5. Why was Peter singled out by the angel?
6. How did the people react when they were told that Jesus had come back to life?
7. What command does Jesus give his disciples with regard to his teachings?
8. What will happen to those who reject the message?
9. What miracles will believers be able to perform?

LUKE

Jesus is the divine-human Savior in the Third Gospel. Modern readers find Luke's narrative the nearest thing to biography among the four Gospels, and many claim they see the man Jesus more clearly portrayed by Luke than by any other evangelist. The work emphasizes the universal extent of Jesus' mercy and compassion, reaching out to encompass Samaritans, women, and Gentiles, none of whom were permitted into the inner courts of the Temple of the Lord in Jerusalem. Luke traces Jesus' genealogy back to Adam in contrast to Matthew who went back only to Abraham — another indication of the universality of this Gospel.

Luke has been identified as a physician who was a Gentile convert to Christianity and a friend of Saint Paul (Col. 4:14; II Tim. 4:11; Philem. 24). If he was the author of this Gospel, as early tradition suggests, then he is also the author of the Acts of the Apostles, since both the Gospel and the Acts are addressed to a man named Theophilus (Luke 1:3; Acts 1:1) and reflect the hand of the same author. No precise dating is possible, and various scholars have set it between A.D. 60 and 90.

THE MIRACULOUS ASPECTS OF THE
BIRTHS OF JOHN AND CHRIST
THE FUNCTION OF THE HOLY SPIRIT
(Luke 1–2)

1. What was miraculous about the birth of John?
2. What was miraculous about the birth of Christ?
3. Describe the attributes of the child promised to Mary.
4. What made Elizabeth's baby "leap in her womb" (1:39–45)? Why does she call Mary "blessed amongst women"?
5. Why did Elizabeth say, "The mother of my Lord has come to me," even though Mary was not yet a mother, and was Elizabeth's cousin?
6. What promise had been given to Simeon by God? How was the promise kept?
7. Jesus was circumcised. What does this tell us about the religion of his parents?
8. What is the first sign that Jesus was more than an ordinary person?
9. Did Jesus think that he was The Son of God? Use the text to back up your argument.
10. What is the role of the Holy Spirit in chapters 1–2?

MIRACLES OF CHRIST
THE GOOD SAMARITAN
PRAYER
THE RICH FOOL
(Luke 5; 10:25–37; 11:5–13, 27–28; 12:13–21)

1. List the miracles of Christ mentioned in chapter 5. What does each miracle demonstrate about Jesus' authority and power?
2. What is the moral of the story about the Good Samaritan?
3. What must one do to insure an answer from God when one prays (11:5–13)?

4. With whom is Jesus most pleased (11:27–28)?
5. What is the moral of the story about the rich fool?

THE PRODIGAL SON
THE RICH MAN AND LAZARUS
THE UNJUST JUDGE
ZACCHAEUS
(Luke 14:33; 15:3–7, 11–32; 16:19–31; 18:1–8; 19:1–10)

1. What common moral do the parables of the lost sheep and the prodigal son share?
2. Jesus says that one must forsake all to follow him (14:33). What does he mean by this?
3. What is the moral of the story of the rich man and Lazarus?
4. Why couldn't the rich man be saved? Which biblical principle did he violate?
5. What is the moral of the story of the unjust judge?
6. What made Zacchaeus repent?

THE DEATH AND RESURRECTION OF CHRIST
(Luke 22–24)

1. Jesus and his disciples celebrated the Passover. At that time, Jesus identified himself with the sacrificial lamb. What was he prophesying?
2. Why did Jesus heal the officer's ear?
3. Why was one thief saved, while the other was not?
4. How did Jesus prove that he was not a ghost?
5. What promise did Jesus give his disciples before he returned to heaven?

JOHN

Matthew traced Jesus' origins back to Abraham, and Luke traced him back to Adam, but John transports his readers back to the beginning of all things, that realm of primeval mystery in which the Word that was with God and was God existed. That Word "became flesh and dwelt among us, full of grace and truth; we beheld his glory, glory as of the only Son from the Father" (1:14 RSV). So Jesus is presented as God, come to earth—"pleased as man with men to dwell."

Throughout, there is a sublime, elevated quality to the book. Discourses by Jesus and the Evangelist (it is frequently difficult to determine where Jesus' remarks end and the author's comments begin) abound in the text and are characterized by the symbolic use of terms like "water," "light," "bread," "door," "shepherd," "life," and "way."

In this Gospel, the author makes specific reference to himself, speaking of "the disciple whom Jesus loved . . . who has written these things" (21:20, 24 RSV). Tradition holds that since the disciple whom Jesus loved is commonly associated in the narrative with Simon Peter, he must be the apostle John. In the Synoptic Gospels, Peter, James, and John were almost invariably grouped together as the inner circle of Jesus' disciples. The Acts record the early death of James (Acts 12:1-2), leaving John as the only candidate of the three to supply the identity of the nameless disciple whom Jesus loved.

The date of John's Gospel was for years hotly disputed, some scholars arguing that its elevated content could not have been the product of the primitive first-century church, asserting that it must have been written perhaps as late as A.D. 200. Then, in 1934, C. H. Roberts, Fellow of St. John's College, Oxford (England), was sorting through some papyrus fragments that had been acquired years before by Bernard Grenfell in Egypt and which now belonged to the John Rylands Library at the University of Manchester, England. Suddenly he noticed that one of the fragments, a piece measuring only 2½ by 3½ inches, contained several sentences from John's Gospel (18:31–33, 37–38). From the style of the writing, Roberts dated the fragment between A.D. 100 and 150, and many eminent paleographers (men who specialize in the art or science of deciphering ancient writings) agree with his conclusions.

The traditional birthplace of the Fourth Gospel was the city of Ephesus in Asia Minor (Turkey), and for that document to have been copied and circulated as far as the Nile Valley by A.D. 150 is compelling evidence that its original date of composition could be set before the end of the first century (*ca.* A.D. 90).

JESUS IS GOD
WATER INTO WINE
YOU MUST BE BORN AGAIN
(John 1–3)

1. Who is the Word? Give evidence from the text that John believed that Jesus is God.
2. In what sense does Jesus, the Lamb of God, take away the sins of the world? Relate this to the Old Testament sacrificial system.
3. Why is "light" a good symbol for Christ?
4. Why did Jesus perform the miracle at Cana?
5. Jesus "knew what was in man" (2:23–25). What does this mean?
6. How can a person be born again?
7. Why are some people condemned, according to Jesus in chapter 3?
8. How is the Spirit of God like the wind?

THE SAMARITAN WOMAN
HEALING AT THE POOL OF BETHESDA
THE BREAD OF LIFE
THE WOMAN TAKEN IN ADULTERY
RAISING OF LAZARUS
(John 4:1-42; 5:1-16, 19-30; 6:32-59; 8:1-11; 11:1-44)

1. In what sense did Jesus give the Samaritan woman "living water"?
2. Why did Jesus heal the man at the pool of Bethesda?
3. According to 5:19-30, what authority has God given to Jesus? Why?
4. In what sense is Jesus the "bread of life"?
5. What lesson did Jesus teach the people who were ready to stone the woman taken in adultery?
6. Contrast Jesus' way of dealing with adultery with that of Moses.
7. Jesus said, "I am the resurrection and the life" (11:1-44). What did he mean by this?

JUDAS
HUMILITY
A PROMISE OF MANSIONS
THE TRUE VINE
DOUBTING THOMAS
(John 12-17, 20)

1. How did Judas reveal his greed in chapter 12?
2. What lesson did Jesus teach his disciples by washing their feet (13:1-17)?
3. What comforting promise did Jesus give his disciples regarding the afterlife?
4. Who is the Comforter in 14:15-31? What is his job? When will he arrive? (Read 16:5-16 also.)
5. If Jesus is the vine, and his followers are the branches, who is the gardener? What happens to the branches when

they are disconnected from the vine? Relate this to Jesus and his followers.

6. How did Jesus convince Thomas of his resurrection? What did Jesus mean by "blessed are those who have not seen and yet believe"?

7. John states his purpose for writing the Gospel in chapter 20. What is it?

Doubting Thomas: The term "doubting Thomas" originated with the gospel story found in John 20:24–29. Thomas wanted to see before he would believe. Today, the phrase is used of anyone who is skeptical.

The Acts of the Apostles

Continuing the story of Luke's Gospel, the Book of Acts takes its reader through the history of the early church, from the day of Jesus' ascension to the time when Paul the Apostle was proclaiming and teaching about the kingdom of God in Rome itself. The progress of the book is chiefly geographical: opening in Jerusalem, the word spread north into Samaria (8:5), out to the coastal plain (8:40), northward again to Damascus (9:10), Antioch, and Cyprus (11:19), and Asia Minor (13:13). From there, the direction shifted to the west as Paul and his band crossed over to Macedonia and down into Greece (Achaia) (16:11). The final chapters include a storm-tossed voyage across the Mediterranean, ending in shipwreck on a shoal in the mouth of a bay on the island of Malta. From there the Apostle traveled to Rome (28:16).

In the latter part of the book, much of the narrative is in the first person "we," rather than in the third person "he" or "they." The common explanation for this is that the author, Luke (see the introduction to the Gospel of Luke for questions of authorship and date), was an eyewitness to the events narrated in the first person and quite naturally included himself in the text.

122

THE COMING OF THE HOLY SPIRIT
ANANIAS AND SAPPHIRA
PETER AND JOHN CONTINUE THE WORK
OF CHRIST
(Acts 1–5)

1. What are Jesus' final instructions to his disciples before he ascends to heaven?
2. Describe the coming of the Holy Spirit as narrated in chapter 2. Why is this called the "Pentecostal experience"?
3. Peter knows exactly what is happening when his friends begin speaking in strange languages. What is his explanation?
4. What statement of Jesus (before he ascended) gave Peter and John the confidence to attempt to cure the crippled man?
5. Why were Ananias and Sapphira punished so severely?
6. Why did the Christians share things in common (Acts 2:42–47)? Why don't they do this today?
7. What advice did Gamaliel give the Sanhedrin concerning the followers of Christ? Why was this good advice?

THE STONING OF STEPHEN
SIMONY
PHILIP AND THE ETHIOPIAN
THE CONVERSION OF SAUL
PETER'S LESSON
(Acts 6–10)

1. Compare Stephen's last moments to Christ's last moments. How were they similar?
2. What does the word "simony" mean? Relate it to the account in Acts 8:9–23.
3. How did Philip help the Ethiopian eunuch?
4. What was Saul's job when he was a Pharisee?

5. Describe Saul's conversion.
6. What lesson does God teach Peter in the vision He shows him?

PETER'S ESCAPE FROM PRISON
HEROD'S DEATH
PAUL AND BARNABAS HONORED
THE MEETING AT JERUSALEM
(Acts 12–15)

1. Describe Peter's escape from prison.
2. How and why did Herod die?
3. Why did the people think Paul and Barnabas were gods?
4. Why were Paul and Barnabas so upset when the people tried to worship them?
5. What were the main conflicts at the meeting of Jerusalem? How were these conflicts resolved?

THE ADVENTURES OF PAUL
(Acts 16, 19, 24, 28)

1. In Acts 16:6–10, the Holy Spirit "tells" Paul not to preach in Asia, but to go to Macedonia instead. What does this tell you about the function of the Holy Spirit?
2. Where do fortune-tellers get their power? Read 16:16–19.
3. What made the jailer want to be "saved"?
4. In 19:11–12, people are healed by anointed handkerchiefs and aprons. Compare this with the teachings of Christ.
5. By what two names were Christians known? (Read chapter 24.)
6. Why did the natives of Malta (28:1 RSV) think Paul was a god?
7. Paul says the Holy Spirit spoke through Isaiah (28:25–28). What function of the Holy Spirit is revealed through this statement?

Fortune-Tellers, Sorcerers, etc.: See the appendix article entitled "Witchcraft."

The Letters of the New Testament

The next section of the New Testament is devoted to the letters (epistles) of Paul, Peter, James, John, and Jude (the letter to the Hebrews is anonymous). Paul's letters are of two sorts: the ones he wrote to various churches, and ones he wrote to individuals. Of those he wrote to individuals, all but one, Philemon, are called "pastoral epistles," because they are comprised mainly of advice and instruction to pastors and church leaders. The remainder of the letters, those of Peter, James, John, and Jude, are called "the catholic epistles" because they are not directed to any specific congregation or named individuals—thus they are regarded as general or universal (catholic).

ROMANS

Paul's letter to the Christians in Rome was probably written while he was living in Corinth (15:25–27; cf. I Cor. 16:3–5) engaged in strenuous missionary activity, as he had been for some years. Part of his work had involved collecting contributions from the churches of Greece and Asia Minor for the relief of the famine-stricken churches of Judea. From Corinth, he would travel to Jerusalem, and from there he had plans for taking the Gospel to Spain, stopping on the way to visit the already-established church in Rome. It was with an eye to introducing himself and his teaching to the Roman Christians that Paul wrote this letter.

The epistle is the closest thing in the entire Bible to a complete theological treatise. Man's sinfulness and the need for man to be made right with God through faith are the themes of the first half of the book; later, the Apostle explores the agony and the implications of the rejection of his Gospel by the larger part of the Jewish community (chaps. 9–11), concluding the book with specific moral application, general exhortations, and greetings.

The date of the letter is between A.D. 54 and 58.

THE THEOLOGY OF THE APOSTLE PAUL
(Rom. 1–8)

1. How can a person know whether or not God exists, according to Paul (chap. 1)?
2. What is the result of rejecting God (chap. 1)?
3. How can man, in his depravity, be reconciled to a just God (chap. 3)?
4. In Romans 4:11–12, Paul calls Abraham the spiritual father of all Christians. What does he mean?
5. Paul discusses the relationship between Adam and Christ (chap. 5). What was the function of Adam? What is the function of Christ?
6. Paul says that death has no more dominion over man. What does he mean by this (chap. 6)?
7. Paul describes a constant struggle between the "spirit" and the "flesh." How can one overcome the "flesh" (chap. 7)?
8. Romans 8:28 says, "All things work together for good to them that love God." How would this philosophy affect a person's attitude toward life in general?

THE FATE OF THE JEWISH NATION
CORRECT CHRISTIAN BEHAVIOR
(Rom. 9–16)

1. Paul grieved over the Jews (chap. 9). Why?
2. Paul says that a partial blessing came from the fact that Israel (the Jews) rejected Christ as the Messiah (chap. 11). What is this blessing?
3. Paul says Israel will eventually be saved (chap. 11). Why?
4. Paul says, "Present your bodies a living sacrifice . . . unto God" (chap. 12). What does he mean?
5. What point does Paul make in 12:3–8?
6. In chapter 14, Paul discusses the subject of "conscience." What is the guideline he gives as to whether or not a person should do a given thing?

I CORINTHIANS

Paul's adventurous but somewhat disappointing mission in Athens (Acts 17:16–34) was followed by a tremendous response to his message in Corinth, an important trade center less than one hundred miles west of Athens (Acts 18:1–18). There he spent more than eighteen months establishing a full-fledged congregation in the face of considerable opposition. Some two to four years later, he wrote to them from Ephesus, just across the Aegean Sea, after hearing of troubles among the flock. Personality divisions, toleration of immorality, and irregularities at the communion table (the church's sacramental memorial of Jesus' death through the elements of bread and wine) were just some of the things that prompted the Apostle's remarks in this epistle.

The content gives us unparalleled insight into the life of a local assembly of Christians in the first century, and it also throws tremendous light upon the personality and thinking of Paul himself. Written prior to his letter to the Romans, this document is dated about A.D. 54.

PAUL'S METHOD OF PREACHING
GOD'S TEMPLE
IMMORALITY
(I Cor. 1-5)

1. With what problem is Paul concerned in chapter 1?
2. Why does Paul call the message he preaches "foolish" (chap. 1)?
3. According to Paul, why does God call people who are not esteemed by the world (chap. 1)?
4. What is the best way to convince people of the existence of God (chap. 2)?
5. Why are some people unable to understand supernatural things?
6. How are Christians "God's temple" (3:16)?
7. Why was the man cast out of the church (chap. 5)?

SEXUAL CONDUCT FOR THE MARRIED
AND UNMARRIED (I Cor. 6-7)

1. Why is it wrong to satisfy one's sexual appetite in the same manner one satisfies one's appetite for food, according to Paul's thinking (chap. 6)?
2. Under what circumstances should a Christian marry?
3. Under what circumstances should a Christian refrain from marrying (chap. 7)?
4. Explain the meaning of 7:3-5. How can this be misinterpreted?
5. Compare Paul's comments on divorce with Christ's (I Cor. 7:12-16; Matt. 19:3-9).

THEOLOGY AND CUSTOM
THE LORD'S SUPPER
(I Cor. 8–11)

1. Under what circumstances should a Christian refuse to eat food offered to a pagan god? Why?
2. Why does a minister deserve support by the church?
3. Paul says women should cover their heads in worship. Why aren't they required to do so today?
4. Paul says it is a shame for a woman to cut her hair (chap. 11). Is this true today?
5. What problem did the early church encounter with regard to the Lord's Supper?
6. What should people do before participating in the Lord's Supper?

Long Hair: In chapter 11, Paul teaches that women should wear a veil during worship, and that to refuse to do so would be so shameful a thing that the offender should shave her head. The veil was a symbol of the woman's submission to her husband, or, if unmarried, to her father. The mention of angels in 11:10 probably reflects the belief that one of their functions is to administer the divine order whereby God delegates his authority downward through a chain-of-command—in this case, through the man to the woman.* If, on another hand, the function of Paul's instruction is to protect women from physical, emotional, and spiritual attack, then the angels may refer to "fallen angels" (demons) who would initiate and press just such attacks.†

If a woman's long hair is her pride, says Paul, the same coiffure for a man would be a disgrace (11:14–15). The Nazirite law of the Old Testament provides for the unhindered growth of a man's hair, but the special nature of that provision in it-

---

* Cf. the discussion of David's subordination to Saul, p. 59. One interesting illustration of this principle is contained in the special rules for women under vows in Numbers 30.

† Cf. the discussion of the devil in the appendix, pp. 157–60.

self indicates that such a practice would be the exception, not the rule. Hair was not considered long until it reached the shoulders.

THE GIFTS OF THE SPIRIT
LOVE
CHURCH ORDER
THE RESURRECTION OF CHRIST
(I Cor. 12–15)

1. Name the nine gifts of the Holy Spirit. Why are these gifts given to people?
2. Why is it foolish to favor one gift over another?
3. What is the point made in chapter 13?
4. What problems come up when the gifts are operating in a church?
5. Why is it necessary to believe in the resurrection of Christ, according to Paul?
6. How does Paul prove that the dead can live again?
7. Paul claims that death is defeated when it comes to claim a Christian. How?

II CORINTHIANS

Paul's second letter to the church at Corinth will provoke some detective work on the part of anyone who wants to read it with understanding. It is largely a response to situations, words, etc., of which we have no immediate knowledge other than what Paul himself says. The reader must try to piece together a picture for himself of exactly what the Apostle is confronting in his response.

Tension had arisen in his relationship with the Corinthian congregation, and apparently this letter, while it still reflects Paul's own anguish over that tension, was written to express the relief he had experienced when his associate, Titus, returned with a report that things were changing for the better in Corinth (7:2–16). Paul was living in Macedonia, and wrote the letter sometime before A.D. 57.

ADVICE TO THE CORINTHIANS
(II Cor. 1–6)

1. In chapter 3, Paul says that as the Jews read the Old Testament, there is a veil over their eyes. What does he mean by this? How can they remove the veil?
2. To whom is the gospel message hidden? Why (chap. 4)?
3. Paul says, "Though our outward man perish, yet the inward man is renewed day by day" (4:16). What does he mean?
4. Paul says that things which are unseen are eternal (4:18). How is this true?
5. According to Paul, what will happen when we appear before the judgment seat of Christ (chap. 5)?
6. Paul says, "For he hath made him to be sin for us, who knew no sin; that we might be made the righteousness of God in him" (5:21). Who was made sin? How?
7. Paul says, "Be ye not unequally yoked together with unbelievers; for what fellowship hath righteousness with unrighteousness? and what communion hath light with darkness?" (6:14). What does Paul mean by this?

ADVICE TO THE CORINTHIAN CHURCH
(II Cor. 7–12)

1. Paul says that although Jesus was rich, he became poor for the sake of the people. How?
2. Explain 9:6–7.
3. In 11:14, Paul says that Satan transforms himself into an angel of light. Give an example of this.
4. In chapters 11–12, Paul tells why he has a right to be proud. What is his reason? Why does he choose not to be proud (not to "glory")?

GALATIANS

Abruptly and unhesitatingly, Paul opens this most intense of all his letters, and the one which was later to stir Martin Luther to challenge all of Christendom with his exposition of its contents. Paul had evangelized in Galatia (a Roman province in central Asia Minor) early in his career (Acts 13:14–14:28). Following the establishment of the church there, other missionaries arrived on the scene, after Paul's departure, who insisted that a Gentile must become a Jew before he could become a Christian, i.e., he must submit to circumcision, and observe the Sabbath and other seasonal holidays of Judaism, keeping the law of Moses. Paul vehemently argues that no such ritual or moral observances can make a man righteous, but that only faith in Christ pleases God.

Dating of the epistle depends on questions related to the Council of Jerusalem (Acts 15), opening a variety of possibilities between A.D. 49 and 56.

THE LAW VERSUS FAITH
(Gal. 1–6)

1. Why does Paul recount his life story, telling of his conversion to Christianity and his entire ministry (chaps. 1–2)?
2. Paul says, "A man is not justified by the works of the law but by the faith of Jesus Christ" (Gal. 2:16). What does he mean?
3. After reading chapter 3, give a definition of the "spirit" and the "flesh."
4. How is Abraham the forefather of the principle of "justification by faith"?
5. What purpose does the law serve (chap. 3)?
6. Paul says, "There is neither Jew nor Greek . . . ye are all one in Christ" (3:28). What does he mean?

7. About what does Paul warn the Galatians in chapters 4–5?
8. What are the works of the flesh, and how can one avoid them (chap. 5)?
9. What is the fruit of the Spirit, and how may one obtain it (chap. 5)?
10. Paul says that a person who "sows to his own flesh" (RSV) will reap corruption (chap. 6). What does he mean? What will happen to one who "sows to the Spirit"?

EPHESIANS

Described by some as the most sublime of Paul's epistles, the letter to the Ephesians is the first in the canonical order of those he wrote while in prison (3:1; 4:1; 6:20), presumably during his two-year imprisonment in Rome, A.D. 59–61 (Acts 28:30). As is common in his letters, the first half is devoted to doctrinal matters and the second to practical. The tone is in stark contrast to the righteous indignation of Galatians; in calm, deliberate fashion, the Apostle touches profoundly on the theme of Christ and the Church.

CHRIST AND THE CHURCH
(Eph. 1–6)

1. According to chapter 1, who is the head of the Church?
2. How can a person be "saved" (chap. 2)?
3. What serves as Christ's body, since Christ is no longer here in the flesh (chap. 1)?
4. Explain 2:13–14.
5. Why did God appoint apostles, prophets, evangelists, pastors, and teachers (chap. 4)?
6. What sins are warned against in chapter 5?
7. What advice does Paul give parents (chap. 6)?
8. Why does a Christian need the spiritual armor described in chapter 6?

PHILIPPIANS

Philippi, an important colonial trade center in Macedonia, was the site of Paul's first missionary effort in Europe (Acts 16). It was a fruitful work, and a leading woman merchant of the vicinity, Lydia, was among those converted. While there, Paul experienced his first imprisonment for the sake of the Gospel he preached.

At the time of writing, the Apostle is in prison (1:12-26), perhaps in Rome, Caesarea, or Ephesus (*ca.* 58-63), and he wishes to acknowledge the gift that the Philippian church had sent him by the hands of Epaphroditus (2:25-29; 4:18). The letter breathes with radiant serenity as the Apostle describes his own response to his incarceration and the possibility of his death.

PAUL'S EXHORTATION TO THE PHILIPPIANS
(Phil. 1-4)

1. Paul says, "The things which happened unto me have fallen out rather unto the furtherance of the gospel" (1:12). What happened to him, and how could it further the Gospel?
2. What is Paul's goal in life?
3. According to Paul, is Christ equal to God (chap. 2)?
4. Paul says, "What things were gain to me those I counted loss for Christ" (3:7). What things did Paul count loss for Christ?
5. Why should a Christian be happy?
6. What should a Christian think about? What effect will this have upon his attitude in general? Why is this good psychology (chap. 4)?

COLOSSIANS

An insignificant town in the district of Phrygia in Asia Minor, Colossae had originally been evangelized by Epaphras, whom Paul had dispatched there. Later, news of false teachers who had come into the new church and disrupted it with their claims of superior "knowledge" in divine matters, urging a mixture of rigorous asceticism and formal ritual (2:16–23), had come to Paul's ears. He now writes to emphasize the pre-eminence of Christ in all things and show that his all-sufficiency made these other things unessential, even heretical.

Like Ephesians and Philippians, this letter was written from a prison cell, probably in the early sixties.

PAUL EXHORTS THE COLOSSIANS
(Col. 1–4)

1. What place does Christ hold in the theology of Paul? Why does he remind the Colossians of this?
2. What does Paul warn them about in chapter 2?
3. Explain the symbolism of baptism in 2:12.
4. What does "principalities and powers" (2:15) mean?
5. Paul says, "Let your speech be alway with grace, seasoned with salt" (4:6). What does he mean?

I THESSALONIANS

Thessalonica was the capital of Macedonia, and it was there that Paul and Silas (Sylvanus) had gone after being asked to leave Philippi. They preached in the synagogue there for three Sabbaths, proclaiming Jesus as the Messiah, and arguing, from the Old Testament, the necessity of his death and resurrection.

Some of the Jews and a large number of Gentile God-fearers *
received Paul's and Silas' word. This success began to annoy
those of the synagogue who were still unpersuaded by the
Apostle's arguments, and they began to accuse him of sedition
before the local authorities, forcing him finally to depart
(Acts 17).

Concerned for the welfare of the fledgling congregation of
believers in Thessalonica, Paul sent Timothy to encourage
and help them. Timothy's return to Paul in Corinth following
his mission, bringing a good report of their perseverance, was
apparently the occasion for the writing of this epistle (3:1–6).
It is the earliest of Paul's letters known to us, and perhaps
the earliest document of the entire New Testament, written
about the year 50.

PAUL'S ADMONITION TO THE
THESSALONIANS
(I Thess. 1–5)

1. With what problems of the Thessalonian church does Paul
   deal in chapter 4?
2. Why is it foolish for Christians to grieve excessively over
   the dead?
3. In 5:1–8, Paul speaks of the Day of the Lord. What does
   he mean?
4. Paul says, "Abstain from all appearance of evil" (5:22).
   What does he mean? Give an example.

---

* Throughout the Mediterranean, Judaism had attracted a sizable portion
of Gentiles into its fold. Many of them were convinced of the truth and reality
of the one God of Israel, but were unwilling to undergo the rite of circumcision,
thereby relegating themselves to the status of God-fearing worshipers who sat
in the rear of the synagogue, not yet in full membership.

II Thessalonians

Paul's second letter to the Thessalonians was motivated by
a false teaching that had arisen in the new church saying that
the Day of the Lord had already come (2:1–2). Both of the
Thessalonian epistles contain a considerable amount of teaching about eschatology (the study of last things) focusing on the
return, or second coming, of Christ.

The second Thessalonian letter was evidently written soon
after the first letter to Corinth.

ADVICE CONCERNING THE SECOND COMING
(II Thess. 1–3)

1. What must happen before Christ returns (2:3–4)?
2. Paul says, "Be not weary in well doing" (3:13). Why does
   he say this?

I Timothy

First Timothy and the two letters that follow it, II Timothy
and Titus, are called the pastoral epistles, because they were
written to pastors, unlike the previous letters which were
addressed to entire congregations. Paul met Timothy during
his second missionary journey (Acts 15:36–16:5) in Lystra, a
town in the district of Galatia. He was already a disciple, the
son of a Jewish woman, Eunice, who was a believer, but his
father was a Greek (Gentile). His identity with regard to the
Jewish community was unclear, and Paul, sensing the problem, took him and circumcised him. After that, Timothy accompanied Paul on his missionary tours for some time, until
he later settled into a permanent pastorate.

Paul's authorship of all the pastoral epistles has been hotly
disputed for some time. The challengers claim that the style

and vocabulary are too unlike that of the other Pauline letters, and that these must be the work of a disciple of Paul, writing under his name as a pseudonym. Defenders of Pauline authorship point to change in circumstances, environment, etc., to explain the changes in style and vocabulary. They are very doubtful about a Christian author using a prestigious pseudonym, no matter how common that practice may have been in ancient times.

Because of the authorship dispute, dates for these letters have been variously set between A.D. 60 and 90.

ADVICE TO A PASTOR
(I Tim. 1–6)

1. What warning does Paul give Timothy (chap. 1)?
2. How does Paul feel about his own righteousness?
3. Paul tells Timothy to pray for governmental authorities. What does this tell you about Paul's view of history?
4. What are the qualifications for a bishop (chap. 3)?
5. How should a younger man go about correcting an older member of the church (chap. 5)? Why?
6. What are the responsibilities of a man toward his family (chap. 3)?
7. What is Paul's view on materialism? Quote from chapter 6.

II TIMOTHY

The second letter to Timothy emphasizes the young pastor's need for personal strength and perseverance in contrast to the first letter with its stress on more general matters of church life. Paul writes from prison and is facing certain martyrdom in Rome where, according to tradition, he was beheaded. For questions of authorship and date, see the introduction to I Timothy.

GUARD AGAINST ERROR
THE END TIMES
(II Tim. 1-4)

1. Paul warns Timothy to refrain from the entanglements of this life (2:1-13). What does he mean by this?
2. Paul says, "Flee also youthful lusts" (2:22). What are youthful lusts?
3. In 3:1-5, Paul gives Timothy a list of signs that the "end times" are near. List the things mentioned by Paul. For each, give your view as to whether or not these signs are present now and whether or not they have always been present.
4. According to Paul, what is the place of the Bible in the life of a believer?
5. How does Paul feel about his coming death? Why?

TITUS

Titus is not mentioned in the Acts, but his career can be pieced together from Paul's other letters, especially II Corinthians and Galatians. A Gentile by birth, he was taken by Paul on the delegation from Antioch to Jerusalem (Gal. 2:1-10) for the council held there regarding the admission of Gentiles to the church. Later, he was sent on missions to Corinth to deal with problems in that unpredictable congregation (II Cor. 7:13-16), and, subsequent to that, was stationed in Crete as a pastor-overseer (Titus 1:5). A final reference (II Tim. 4:10) places him in Dalmatia, a district on the eastern coast of the Adriatic Sea, roughly the same territory occupied by present-day Albania.

For questions of authorship and date, see the introduction to I Timothy.

ADVICE TO TITUS REGARDING SANCTIFICATION
(Titus 1-3)

1. Paul warns Titus about something in chapter 1. What is it?
2. How should family life be conducted (chap. 2)?
3. What is Paul's advice concerning obedience to governmental authorities (chap. 3)?

PHILEMON

This tiny specimen of Paul's epistolary efforts stands last in the collection of his works. It gives unique insight into the writer's deep sensitivity to the intricacies of the human predicament.

While imprisoned in Rome, Paul met a runaway slave named Onesimus, who became a Christian through Paul's efforts. By one of those incredible coincidences, Philemon, Onesimus' former owner, was also a Christian, having been converted under Paul's ministry in Asia Minor. Paul was able to convince Onesimus to return to Philemon, and this letter was sent in conjunction with the slave's return.

Slavery was as much a part of ancient society as trade unionism is of American society, and Roman law stipulated severe penalties for anyone who interfered with the slave-owner's rights. Paul brings together a genuine appreciation for Philemon's rights and a sincere inculcation of principles of the eternal value of every soul and the fraternity of all Christian believers—principles that would lessen the harshness of slavery and ultimately abolish it.

The letter can be dated in the early sixties.

CHRISTIAN BROTHERHOOD
(Philem. 1)

1. Why does Paul call Onesimus, the runaway slave, his child?
2. How is Onesimus, the slave, brother to his master Philemon?
3. Paul says regarding Philemon, "Perhaps he . . . departed for a season that thou shouldest receive him for ever" (1:15). What did he mean by this?
4. What was Paul's relationship to Philemon? Justify your answer by citing specific references from the text.

The Meaning of Onesimus' Name: Verse 11 parenthetically adds, with reference to Onesimus, "Which in time past was to thee unprofitable, but now profitable to thee and to me." The name Onesimus meant "useful" or "profitable," so the use of the words "profitable" and "unprofitable" are a play on the slave's name. Ancient inscriptions and papyrus business documents indicate that the name Onesimus was quite commonly used for slaves.

HEBREWS

It is not even certain that this letter is a letter. The title in the King James Version reads, "The Epistle of Paul the Apostle to the Hebrews," but, in fact, the author nowhere identifies himself in its pages and begins his work more like a treatise or sermon than a letter. Various dates have been assigned between A.D. 60 and 90.

The burden of the book is to demonstrate the superiority of Christianity over Judaism, comparing Christ with angels, Moses, the prophets, Joshua, and the Old Testament priesthood. Christ has in these last days, the author asserts, superseded all those former vehicles for the expression of the Word of God. The title of the book is derived from its extensive references to the practices of Judaism, and from the fact that it was apparently addressed to a group of believers who were in danger of reverting to their former practice of Judaism.

THE PLACE OF CHRIST IN GOD'S PLAN
(Heb. 1–13)

1. Compare the status of Christ to the status of angels.
2. Why did Christ become a man (chap. 2)?
3. Why is Christ greater than Moses (chap. 3)?
4. In what sense is Jesus a high priest (4:14–16; 5:1–10)?
5. How is Melchisedec a type of Christ (Gen. 14:17–20; Heb. 7)?
6. How is Christ's priesthood different from the ordinary priesthood (7:28; 8)?
7. How is Christ a sacrifice as well as a high priest (chap. 9)?
8. Why is the sacrifice of Christ greater than the sacrifice required by Old Testament law (10:1–18)?
9. Chapter 11 lists people who allowed their lives to be ruled by faith. What was the result of this faith?
10. Why does God chastise his followers?

JAMES

Noted for its epigrammatic style and closeness to the Sermon on the Mount (Matt. 5–7), the Letter of James deals with practical and ethical questions, almost to the exclusion of theological doctrine as we know it in Paul's epistles. Martin Luther, whose theology was derived so much from Paul's letters to the Romans and the Galatians, once called this book "an epistle of straw" because of its emphasis that a man is justified by works and not by faith alone (2:24), a concept that seemed to oppose Paul's assertion that a man is justified by faith without works of the law (Gal. 2:16). He failed to perceive the important differences between Paul and James in their presuppositions. To Paul, faith represented the total relationship between the believer and Christ, while for James it meant little more than acceptance of doctrines. When Paul spoke of "works," he meant works of the law that were in opposition to real faith (since those who practiced them did so in an effort to justify themselves before God). James used the term "works" more in the sense that Paul spoke of the fruit of the Spirit (Gal. 5:22). It is inconceivable that Paul would have advocated a faith that did not express itself in a genuinely good life.

James was not the James so frequently associated with Peter and John in the Gospels, for he was martyred very early in the history of the church (Acts 12:2). He may have been the brother of Jesus mentioned in Matthew 13:55 and elsewhere, or it is possible that he was an early church leader otherwise unknown to us. Dates for the epistle have been variously set between A.D. 45 and 95.

FAITH VERSUS WORKS
(James 1–5)

1. Why should a Christian rejoice when tempted?
2. James says, "But be ye doers of the word, and not hearers only, deceiving your own selves" (1:22). Relate this to 2:14.
3. According to James, what is the proof of a person's faith (2:14–26)? Is James saying that a person is saved by his good works?
4. How can one overcome temptation (4:1–7)?
5. Why is the tongue a dangerous member of the body?
6. Explain 4:17 in terms of James' argument about faith and works.
7. What will happen to exploiters (5:1–7)?
8. Faith and works are evident in 5:14–15. How?

I PETER

Although this letter is included in that category of epistles called "catholic," it is nevertheless addressed specifically to

Christians in the northern part of Asia Minor. Considerable persecution was being endured by these believers, and the main intent of the letter is to encourage them in the face of their ordeal.

That Peter is the author of this letter has been difficult for some to accept, because the excellent Greek style in which it is written does not seem to coincide with Peter's reputation for being a bumpkin without much education (Acts 4:13). One explanation offered for this problem is that Peter may have stated his ideas to his secretary, Silvanus, and entrusted the actual composition to him (5:12).

In 5:13 the reference to Babylon is probably a cryptic reference to Rome (cf. Rev. 17, especially v. 9, 18), which was likely the place of the letter's origin. Dates vary between A.D. 60 and 90.

ON CHRISTIAN SUFFERING
(I Pet. 1–5)

1. What moral standard is a Christian responsible for upholding (chap. 1)?
2. How can one become a better Christian (chap. 2)?
3. Peter says of Jesus, "The stone which the builders disallowed, the same is made the head of the corner" (2:7). What did Peter mean?
4. How does Peter feel about obeying the civil law?
5. How can one have a guarantee of longevity?
6. When is it virtuous to suffer (chap. 3)?
7. Who is the enemy of a Christian? How can one overcome him (chap. 5)?
8. Why does God allow the devil to tempt people (chap. 5)?

II PETER

Although this letter claims to have been written by Peter and contains a distinct Petrine autobiographical reference

(1:16), an allusion to a previous letter to the same readers which was very likely I Peter (3:1), and a claim to equal apostolic authority with Paul (3:15–16), it has been argued from early times that such is not the case. The points of argument in this dispute are intricate, having to do with Greek style, the letter's relationship to Jude's epistle, the acceptability of pseudonymous authorship, the opinions of the church fathers of the second, third, and fourth centuries, and the relationship between the early church's expectation of the second coming of Christ and the fall of Jerusalem in A.D. 70. The student who wishes to pursue these questions should refer to books listed in the bibliography.

The content of the letter focuses mainly around the problem of false teachers, and the matter of the apparent delay of the return of Jesus.

THE RETURN OF CHRIST
(II Pet. 1–3)

1. According to chapter 1, how can a person be sure of salvation?
2. According to Peter, who wrote the Bible (chap. 1)?
3. What warning does the author give in chapter 2?
4. Why do some people laugh at the idea of the "second coming" of Christ (chap. 3)?
5. Why does God withhold judgment on the world, even though it is so evil (chap. 3)?
6. When will Christ return (chap. 3)?

I JOHN

This letter and the two that follow it were written anonymously. From early times, however, they have been attributed with great assurance to the pen of the author of the Fourth Gospel, on the basis of the great similarity in style and content between these letters and the Gospel. They are generally dated in the same period as the Gospel, although it is impossible to surmise which came first. They may have circulated as companion pieces.

The purpose of the epistle (it is actually more in the form of a tract or sermon) is to warn its readers against the false teachings of the Gnostics and to urge them to remain faithful to Christ, especially in the exercise of brotherly love. Gnosticism taught the importance of knowledge (Greek *gnosis*), rather than faith, as the vehicle to God. This knowledge was not the kind one receives at college, but an occult knowledge achieved through special supernatural enlightenment. This ethereal emphasis was also demonstrated in Gnosticism's deprecation of the body and elevation of the non-material (*cf.* I John 4:2–3). As much as the Bible speaks of the importance of the spiritual aspect of life, it is nevertheless inconceivable to think of life apart from the body. One never reads in the pages of the Bible a treatise on the immortality of the soul, but there is considerable mention of physical resurrection (*cf.* Ezek. 37 and I Cor. 15). Traditional theology has taught that the spirits of the faithful live in heaven (*cf.* Luke 16:19–31), there awaiting the final day of resurrection when their spirits will be rejoined, not with their old corruptible bodies, but with "spiritual" bodies suited for eternity (I Cor. 15:42–44).

TRUE RIGHTEOUSNESS
(I John 1–5)

1. What is the proof of a true Christian (chap. 1)?
2. What encouragement does John give to the sinner?
3. John says, "If we say that we have not sinned, we make him a liar, and his word is not in us" (1:10). What heresy is John combating with these words?
4. What does John mean by "the world" in 2:15–17?
5. What heresy is John combating in 2:22?
6. How should a true Christian behave toward other Christians (chap. 3)?

7. How can one overcome the world (chap. 5)?
8. When can one be guaranteed of an answer to his prayer (chap. 5)?
9. What theme dominates this book?

II JOHN

This very brief letter is addressed to "the elect lady and her children," which most scholars have understood to mean an unnamed congregation and its members, although some take it less figuratively to mean a woman of elevated status who was a believer. The letter itself echoes much of I John, with a warning against giving hospitality to false teachers lest one become a sharer in their wicked work.

For questions of authorship and dating, see the introduction to I John.

WARNING AGAINST FALSE TEACHERS
(II John 1)

1. Of what does John remind the church in verses 5–6? Why is this so important for Christians?
2. Describe the false teaching being opposed in this letter.

III JOHN

Unlike the two previous Johannine letters, this one is addressed to a specific individual, Gaius, who is urged to continue in his friendly support of itinerant missionaries. The letter was apparently provoked by the behavior of a certain Diotrophes of the same church who was refusing to acknowledge the writer's authority and who was putting the missionaries out of the church.

For questions of authorship and date, see the introduction to I John.

A PLEA TO THE CHURCH
(III John 1)

1. For what does the writer commend Gaius?
2. Enumerate Diotrophes' misdeeds.
3. Drawing from the text in general, give your impression of any implications John may be drawing about Diotrophes' morality.

JUDE

The author of this epistle introduces himself as Jude, a servant of Jesus Christ and brother of James. He was probably, as tradition affirms, the same Jude mentioned in Mark 6:3 as one of the brothers of Jesus. Some have argued that the book is pseudonymous, but it seems unlikely that the author would have chosen such a relatively obscure name for his pseudonym. The letter may be dated about the year 80.

The purpose of the letter is to warn against false teachers who are identified not so much by what they teach as by how they live. Jude crisply denounces them, and his letter virtually bristles with one of the fullest sets of defamatory accusations to be found anywhere in the Bible.

WARNINGS AGAINST FALSE TEACHERS
(Jude 1)

1. What is Jude's stated purpose in writing this letter?
2. Describe the false teachers he attacks.
3. What positive direction does the author give his readers after warning them to avoid the heretics?

The Revelation

The book of Revelation is the New Testament's only specimen of apocalyptic literature. It is filled with a variety of
images and pictures that are meant to make a powerful appeal
to the reader's imagination. It is an appropriate book with
which to close the Bible, focusing as it does on the final con-
summation of the world when the "kingdom of the world has
become the kingdom of our Lord and of his Christ, and he
shall reign for ever and ever" (11:15 RSV).

The author is John (1:1,4,9; 22:8), who was in exile at the
time he saw the visions contained in this book, on the desolate
isle of Patmos in the Aegean Sea, by the order of Emperor
Domitian, who ruled the Roman empire A.D. 81–96. Tradition identifies this John with the author of the Gospel of John,
but there is no conclusive evidence that he was. If the apostle
John authored the Gospel, the three letters, and this apocalypse,
then it is strange that the latter is the only one to which he
affixed his name. (See p. 6.)

The book of Revelation contains many symbols and apocalyptic figures. Numerical symbols abound, along with strange
beasts, a harlot seated upon a beast, and a woman with child
clothed with the sun. The keys to unlock the meaning of many
of these symbols have simply been lost to us; others should be
plain to any historically informed reader (e.g., to properly
interpret 17:9 one needs to know that Rome was, and is, a
city built on seven hills); and still others can be penetrated by
comparison with Old Testament apocalyptic symbolism such as
is found in Daniel and Ezekiel.

THE VISION OF CHRIST
THE SEVEN CHURCHES
(Rev. 1–3)

1. Where is John when he writes the book of Revelation? Why is he there?
2. Prove by symbolism that it is Jesus whom John sees in his vision.
3. List the seven churches and the major fault of each.

THE TWENTY-FOUR ELDERS AND THE
FOUR BEASTS
THE SEALED SCROLL
THE SEALS
(Rev. 4–6)

1. What do the twenty-four elders symbolize?
2. What do the "eyes" of the beasts symbolize?
3. What function do the elders and the beasts serve?
4. The scroll is sealed with seven seals (chap. 5). What does the number seven symbolize?
5. Who is worthy to open the seals? Why?
6. Why do the elders and the beasts worship Christ?
7. What happens when each of the first six seals is opened?

THE 144,000
THE SEVENTH SEAL
THE BITTER-SWEET SCROLL
(Rev. 7–10)

1. What do the 144,000 symbolize?
2. Why is there an interlude before the opening of the seventh seal?
3. What happens when each of the seven angels blows his trumpet in chapters 8–9?

4. Why is the scroll sweet to the mouth and bitter to the stomach (chap. 10)? Explain the symbolism.

THE ARK OF THE COVENANT
THE WOMAN AND THE MANCHILD
THE BEAST AND THE DRAGON
THE MYSTERIOUS NUMBER 666
THE GRAPES OF WRATH
(Rev. 11–14)

1. What is the Ark of the Covenant? Why is it mentioned here (chap. 11)?
2. Who are the woman, the manchild, and the dragon in chapter 12? Explain the symbolism.
3. What happens to the devil? What "time" is this — past, present, or future of John's writing (chap. 12)?
4. What do the features of the beast with ten horns and seven heads symbolize (chap. 13)?
5. What does the beast who speaks like a dragon but has horns like a lamb symbolize (chap. 13)?
6. What does the number 666 stand for?
7. What does the squeezing of the grapes symbolize?

THE SEVEN GOLDEN BOWLS
BABYLON, THE GREAT WHORE
(Rev. 15–18)

1. What is contained in each of the seven golden bowls?
2. What happened after the pouring out of the seventh bowl?
3. Who is "Babylon, the Great Whore"? Why is Babylon used as the symbol?
4. What is Babylon's main offense against God?

THE MARRIAGE SUPPER OF THE LAMB
THE FATE OF THE DEVIL
THE BOOK OF LIFE
HEAVEN
(Rev. 19–22)

1. What is the marriage supper of the Lamb? Who are the bride, groom, etc. (chap. 19)?
2. What happens to the beast and his followers?
3. What happens to the devil for 1,000 years (chap. 20)?
4. Who sits on the throne? What is contained in the books? By what standard is each man judged? Who is flung into the lake of fire (chap. 20)?
5. What is the New Jerusalem, and who will not be allowed to enter (chap. 21)?
6. Describe heaven. What does each part of the description symbolize?
7. How would you communicate the concept of heaven to a dog? Relate this to how heaven is communicated to man.
8. What happens to those who read the message of Revelation (chap. 22)?
9. What happens to those who tamper with the message?
10. What is the purpose of the book of Revelation?

Appendix
Special Studies

The following topics are included to meet the interest and curiosity expressed by many students. No attempt has been made here to exhaust the biblical references to a given topic. That purpose can better be served by consulting *The Zondervan Topical Bible* or *Strong's Concordance* (see bibliography).

Some of the topics include a set of questions for inductive study. Read the biblical reference carefully, then answer the questions.

MODERN ISRAEL

Today there is much talk of fulfilled prophecy in Jewish as well as Christian circles. During the nineteenth century, a movement began to stir throughout the Diaspora (the community of Judaism scattered among the nations of the world outside Palestine). That movement came to be called Zionism, because it advocated a return of the Jews to their original homeland. Zion was the hill in Jerusalem on which the Temple was built. It later became a symbol for Judaism's claim to the whole territory of Palestine.

The whole period of the Diaspora (587 B.C.–A.D. 1948) was fraught with troubles for the Jews. The book of Esther tells of attempted persecution under Xerxes I (485–464 B.C.) in the Persian empire, but at least there was a partial restoration of Jewish population in Judea until A.D. 70 when Roman legions brought terrific devastation upon the whole countryside, besieged and destroyed Jerusalem and its Temple, and issued an edict forbidding the Jews ever to re-enter the city.

Jews migrated everywhere in the world after that, and there are synagogues in the Far East that trace their origins far back into history. Most Jews, however, resided in Europe and the Middle East, and prospered in many ways in their new homes. Since the Bible forbade the taking of interest on money between brethren (Lev. 25:35–38), the inhabitants of Christendom were generally forbidden to engage in banking. This prohibition did not apply to the Jews, and they could loan at interest to the Christians, who were not their brethren, without violating the commandment. So the Jews became the bankers of Europe and often rose to high positions of court and commercial life.

Nevertheless, the Jews were still isolated in ghettos and frequently subjected to ill-treatment. During the era of the great crusades to regain the Holy Land from the Turks, crusaders in their treks across Europe on the way to the Near East would invade Jewish ghettos in their path and ravage the unbelievers in their midst before turning their swords on the Saracens. Later, in the fourteenth century, successive epidemics of bubonic plague, called the "Black Death," swept across Europe, reducing the population of Northern Europe by 25 percent. Many saw the hand of God against Christendom for its sins in this terrible devastation, but others were quick to accuse the Jews of poisoning the wells.

One of the wealthiest and most prestigious Jewish communities of Western Europe were the Sephardim of Spain and Portugal. It is doubtful that any segment of the Diaspora of the Middle Ages achieved the cultural attainments of the Sephardic community. Yet Ferdinand and Isabella evicted the Jews from the Iberian peninsula the same year they dispatched Columbus to America. Most of the Sephardim migrated to the Near East and up into Russian territory. Even today, Spain has only a tiny Jewish community.

As an aftermath of the eighteenth century "enlightenment," great liberal movements swept Western Europe, especially

Germany and France, in the nineteenth century after the end of the Napoleonic wars. These reached their high-water mark in the revolutions of 1848, after which time the pendulum swung solidly toward the right. Since Jews had been often in the forefront of liberal activism, persecution drove many of them to America, where some of the most eminent Jewish businessmen, like Meyer Guggenheim and Adam Gimbel, began their careers as peddlers.

The story in Russia was a sadder one. There revolutionary sentiment was also fermenting, but where the governments of Western Europe found grace to bow a bit to liberal demands, the Czar's government stiffened in reactionary fear. One of the great necessities of this policy was that of somehow siphoning off the growing pressure of the revolutionary spirit as it spread among the peasants. The answer was anti-Semitism. Everywhere, government propaganda placarded the Jews as the true oppressors of the Russian people, in league with the German factory-owners, the English, the Japanese, and the Poles — all hated enemies of Russia. Thus began the fearful pogroms as the organized hoodlums of the Union of Russian People galloped on horseback through the Pale (that district of twenty-five provinces in central Russia where Jews were largely settled) burning, pillaging, raping, and killing. Jewish children were ousted from the schools, and Jewish property was confiscated. This program of persecution drove literally millions of Russian Jews to the shores of America between 1880 and 1920.

Meanwhile in England, another significant development was taking shape. Chaim Weizmann, a Russian Jew, devised a process for synthesizing acetone, an essential ingredient for the production of an explosive. His contribution to the British war effort brought him into contact with important government officials, including Winston Churchill, then First Lord of the Admiralty. Weizmann was an ardent Zionist. The experience of his people in the Diaspora, and especially the pogroms, had convinced him and many other Jewish leaders that there was no solution apart from a sovereign Jewish state, preferably in Palestine, where Jews could live in peace and security. Weizmann was able to win the sympathies of a number of his friends in high government circles toward his Zionist ideas. This sympathy, combined with the political exigencies of World War I, produced the Balfour Declaration, a hand-written note from Foreign Secretary Balfour to Lord Roths-child, the banking magnate and President of the British Zion-ist Federation, that read:

Dear Lord Rothschild,

I have much pleasure in conveying to you, on behalf of His Maj-esty's Government, the following declaration of sympathy with Jewish Zionist aspirations which has been submitted to, and approved by, the Cabinet. His Majesty's Government view with favour the es-tablishment in Palestine of a national home for the Jewish people, and will use their best endeavours to facilitate the achievement of this object, it being clearly understood that nothing shall be done which may prejudice the civil and religious rights of existing non-Jewish communities in Palestine, or the rights and political status enjoyed by Jews in any other country. I should be grateful to you if you would bring this declaration to the knowledge of the Zionist Federation.

That same year, 1917, General Allenby's troops took Jeru-salem from the Turks, who were then allies of Germany. After the war, Palestine became a British mandate and was opened to Jewish immigration.

The Nazi holocaust of World War II was the final catalyst for the establishment of modern Israel. An estimated six million Jews perished in the slave-labor extermination camps of Germany, Poland, and Romania. This enormous barbarism outraged the Western world and won terrific support for Zion-ism, especially in America, where President Harry S. Truman lent the support of his office and prestige to the cause of Zion-ism, though it aroused bitter anti-American resentment among the Arabs and deeply strained British-American relations.

On May 14, 1948, in the midst of unimaginable political and military chaos, David Ben-Gurion gathered his cabinet in the art museum of the city of Tel-Aviv to proclaim the independence of the Republic of Israel. That same day, Harry Truman extended immediate recognition to the new state and buoyed Israeli morale for the war they would have to fight against the Arab nation to make good their claim on the land. In a unique event of history, the descendants of an ancient people reclaimed their homeland and established it as a sovereign state after 2,536 years of subjugation.

Was this a fulfillment of biblical prophecy? Certainly no other political event of the twentieth century has created as much stir and discussion in the religious community, Jewish and Christian, as has this one. Many repudiate the claim of fulfilled prophecy, disdainful of such naïve ideas; others are utterly convinced that this was God's doing and wonderful in their sight. Many, perhaps most, are not nearly so convinced as either of these groups, but they find it a deeply intriguing question.

For further reading:

Solomon Grazel, *A History of the Jews,* rev. ed. (Philadelphia: The Jewish Publication Society of America, 1968).

Howard M. Sachar, *The Course of Modern Jewish History* (Cleveland: The World Publishing Company, 1958).

THE DEVIL

Interest in Satanic matters has risen to major public proportions in the last third of the twentieth century, perhaps more than at any time since the eighteenth century. This article, and the one which follows it, will focus on the biblical background of the matter, to give the reader an understanding of the ancient sources of the contemporary phenomenon.

The serpent in the Garden of Eden (Gen. 3), not fully identified as a personification of the devil until Revelation 12:9, is the traditional first appearance of the great adversary of God and mankind, although he is pictured elsewhere as an angelic being who fell in rebellion against God before the creation of the world (Ezek. 28:11ff.; Isa. 14:12ff.).

The name "Satan" is a direct transliteration of the Hebrew and means "adversary." It is used as a proper name in I Chronicles 21, Job 1-2, Psalm 109, and Zechariah 3, and, transliterated into Greek (*satanos*), it occurs frequently in the New Testament.

The most common appellation in the New Testament is "devil," from the Greek *diabolos* (whence our English "diabolic") meaning "slanderer" or "(false) accuser." This term occurs in thirteen of the twenty-seven books of the New Testament. One interesting term for the prince of demons that occurs only in the Synoptic Gospels, although it is apparently drawn from Hebrew, is "Beelzebub" (*e.g.,* Matt. 12:24) which means, "lord of the flies." The word "evil" (Greek *poneros*) occasionally occurs as a proper name, as in Matthew 13:38 (RSV, the evil one).

Elsewhere the devil is referred to, variously, as the enemy (Matt. 13:39), the tempter (Matt. 4:3), the prince of this world (John 12:31), the god of this world (II Cor. 4:4), the father of lies (John 8:44), an angel of light (a disguise) (II Cor. 11:14), the prince of the power of the air (Eph. 2:2), the great dragon and that old serpent (Rev. 12:9), and the prince of demons (Matt. 12:24 RSV).

When the term devil is used in the plural, as in the King James Version, it refers to demons or evil spirits. In the Old Testament, this is derived from two terms, the first, *sair* (Hebrew), means "satyr" or "demon" with the specific image in mind of the he-goat, or man's torso atop a goat's limbs. In two occurrences, II Chronicles 11:15 and Leviticus 17:7, this word is used as a name for idols. The other term is *shed,* a loanword from the Assyrian *shedu,* meaning, "a protecting spirit." Psalm 106:37 ascribes the practice of human sacrifice of children (a Canaanite practice, Deut. 18:9-12) as being made to and inspired by these devils.

The habitat of demons is among ruins in desolate places that have felt the stroke of God's judgment (Lev. 16:10; Isa. 34:13-14). The New Testament speaks of demonic inhabitation and possession of human beings (Mark 5:1-20) and of their wandering in waterless places upon being expelled from their former home in the person whom they had possessed (Matt. 12:43). These waterless places where the demon spirits found no rest are more fully described in the letters of Paul as "heavenly places" (Eph. 6:12 RSV – the King James Version reads "high places") by which was probably meant the atmosphere surrounding the earth.

The Greek term *daimonion* (*daimon* – a less frequently used cognate) is the direct source of our English word "demon" and is the term that generally stands behind the phrase "a devil" or "devils" in the King James text. In ancient Greece, *daimonion* referred to any non-specified deity; the muses (source of our word "music") were demons who, according to Greek tradition, gave inspiration to poets and songwriters. Obviously, Hellenistic society did not regard demons with the same abhorrence that the biblical writers exhibited toward them.

With this cursory examination of the subject, the reader is now provided with a set of readings and questions by which he may pursue this matter in greater detail.

(Ezek. 28:12–19)

1. What position did Satan hold before he fell?
2. What was his sin?
3. What was his punishment?
4. What does "thou shalt be a terror" (28:19) mean?
5. What was Satan's moral condition before he fell?

(Isa. 14:12–15)

1. Satan was called Lucifer, "day star," before he sinned. Relate his name to his moral position before he sinned.
2. What was his sin as described by Isaiah?
3. What was his punishment?

(Luke 10:18)

According to Luke 10:18, Jesus saw Satan fall like lightning from the sky.

1. When do you think this happened?
2. When did the devil appear on earth the first time?
3. How could Jesus have seen him fall?
4. What is Jesus saying about himself?

THE ROLE OF SATAN
(I Pet. 5:8–9)

1. What does Satan want to do to mankind?
2. How can one avoid the snare of Satan?

(Rev. 2:7–17)

1. What is Satan's function with regard to the faith of God's people?

(Matt. 8:28–34)

1. Prove that Jesus is more powerful than the devil.

RESISTING SATAN
(Eph. 4:26–27; 6:11; James 4:7; I Pet. 5:8)

1. How can a person resist Satan?

WITCHCRAFT

The whole area of sorcery, divination, wizardry, and magic — commonly known as the occult — is directly related to the area of Satan and demons. The various practitioners of the magic arts claim ability to exercise the power of spirits, which they do not regard as evil, in order to perform miracles, divine the future, and influence the lives of men. Such occult activities were regarded as "abominations to the Lord" in the Bible (Deut. 18:9–12), and the punishment for practicing them was death (Exod. 22:18). Although occultism has enjoyed a perennial popularity, its current revival in the United States has reached such proportions that Ouija boards have passed Monopoly as America's fastest-selling game.

Within occultism itself, the various subdivisions of activity are innumerable, and in ancient times the same thing was true, as the biblical lists of prohibitions show (Deut. 18:9–12). The definitions of soothsayer, necromancer, enchanter, witch, clairvoyant, medium, wizard, astrologer, stargazer, fortune-teller, diviner — the list could go on almost indefinitely — are bound to overlap. Many of the terms used to tag occult practices are attached by the opponents of those practices, others are those used by their proponents; synonyms seem at first to be all that these words amount to, and yet the initiated claim to understand subtle but significant shades of difference in every one of them.

The following study examines three passages wherein occult practitioners meet face to face with biblical characters. To answer the questions, it will be necessary to consult a dictionary for specific definitions of occult terms.

(I Sam. 28:7–20)

1. Why was the witch of Endor afraid to bring up the spirit of Samuel the prophet for Saul?

2. How do you know that the witch brought Samuel up?
3. What advice did Saul hope to hear? What did he hear?
4. Prove that the witch of Endor was a necromancer.

(Acts 16:16–18)

1. What does "soothsaying" mean here?
2. Why was Paul annoyed that the girl followed him?
3. Paul commanded the spirit of divination to come out of the girl. What authority did he use? What does this tell you about the authority structures of supernatural beings?

(Acts 8:9–13)

1. What was Simon able to do?
2. Who was glorified as a result of Simon's magic, Simon or God?
3. How can one tell whether a person is performing a miracle by the power of Satan or God?
4. Who, in the book of Exodus, performed a miracle by the power of Satan (Exod. 7:10–13)?

THE END OF THE WORLD

The formal name for the academic study of the end of the world is "eschatology" (Greek *eschatos*—farthest, last—and *logos*—word, study). In every age, this topic has fascinated people from every walk of life who want to know about the future and whether the "signs of the end" forecast in the Bible might not correspond with current events. During the era of the Second World War, many speculated that Adolf Hitler and Benito Mussolini were the beast and the false prophet of the book of Revelation (16:13; 19:20).

Eschatology frequently dominates those books of the Bible with a strong apocalyptic flavor like Ezekiel, Daniel, and Revelation, although it would be difficult to name more than a half-dozen books of the Old or the New Testaments that were devoid of eschatological data. The study that follows is therefore very piecemeal, hitting only significant highlights.

It will be helpful to understand something of the nature of traditional Jewish eschatology as it developed in the inter-testamental period (roughly 350 B.C. to A.D. 20). Since God had created the world in six days and rested on the seventh, it seemed only appropriate to view all of history as passing through six great epochs in order to arrive at the seventh, the age of perfection and rest when Messiah would reign throughout the world. In Galatians 1:4 Paul speaks of "this present evil world" using the Greek term *aion* (our word, "aeon") which is better translated "age" than "world." It is apparent from this that Paul did not regard the present age as the final and golden one, but was looking for "the world (age) to come" of which Jesus also spoke (*e.g.,* Matt. 12:32).

The early church regarded the advent of Jesus as marking the commencement of the last days of the present evil age. Peter, in making his explanation of the strange phenomena of the Day of Pentecost, drew upon the prophecy of Joel that was intended for the last days (Joel 2:28–32; Acts 2:14–21). The writer of Hebrews reflects this same attitude when he speaks of Jesus' appearance having been once for all at the end of the age (Heb. 9:26).

This understanding of Jewish eschatology also casts light upon the use of the expression "eternal life" that occurs so frequently in Johannine literature and elsewhere in the New Testament. The Greek word for eternal was *aionios* from the stem meaning "age"; what was promised was "aeonic" life, which certainly meant life that continued forever without death, but also bespoke that quality of life in the age to come when Messiah would reign.

(Luke 21:7–18)

1. List eight signs of the end-times. Give an example for each one, either to prove that the sign is now happening or that the sign has already happened and is always happening in the world.

(Matt. 24)

1. List two signs of the end-times not mentioned in Luke 21.

(II Tim. 3:1–5)

1. List eleven signs of the end-times. Argue that these signs are always present, or that these signs are increasingly present now.

(Acts 2:17)

1. What is meant by "pour out my Spirit"?
2. What will happen when God "pours out his Spirit"?
3. In your opinion, is this feasible? If so, when?

(Dan. 12:4)

1. List two additional signs of the end-times. Give an example to show that each has already been recently fulfilled. Then argue the contrary.

(II Pet. 3:3–16)

1. How much preparation will one have for the end-times?

(Isa. 35:1)

1. What desert is being referred to?
2. When could one say that prophecy was "fulfilled"? Argue the contrary.

JUDGMENT DAY

The prophets of the Old Testament spoke repeatedly of the Day of the Lord (Isa. 13:6; Jer. 46:10; Ezek, 30:3; Joel 1:15; Amos 5:20; Zeph. 1:14). Often this referred to the imminent catastrophe they foresaw coming upon the people as punishment for national sin and rebellion. In this way, the fall of Jerusalem in 587 B.C. was the Day of the Lord, and yet there is a brooding sense among their proclamations that there would be, further off, a great and final Day of the Lord.

By the first century of the Christian era, this idea had fixed itself quite firmly in Jewish thinking, especially among the influential Pharisees (Acts 23:8). In answering the following questions, note the reference you use for each from among the list of nine provided.

(Matt. 11:20-24; 25; John 5:22; Rom. 2:12-16; I Cor. 6:2-3; II Cor. 5:10; Heb. 9:27; II Pet. 3:7; Rev. 20:11-15)

1. What will happen to those who work for Christ without helping the man who is "down and out"?
2. Who will be judged on judgment day?
3. By what standard will man be judged?
4. What record does God have of man's deeds?
5. What punishment is reserved for the sinner?
6. When is judgment day?
7. How can one escape eternal punishment?

HELL

Closely associated with the question of judgment is that of the precise nature of judgment. What will be the final fate of the wicked? The book of Revelation promises a lake of fire for those whose names were not found written in the Lamb's book of life (20:15), an idea which finds its roots in the Old Testament, where fire is a common vehicle of expression for the wrath of God (e.g., Ps. 79:5).

The Hebrew word behind the translation "hell" in the Old Testament of the King James Version is *sheol,* which means "the pit, the grave, the underworld." It is the place whither men descend at death (Gen. 37:35) and into which Korah and his associates plummeted alive (Num. 16:30–33). Isaiah personified it as an insatiable monster (28:15,18). It was a dark, gloomy place from which there was no return (Job 17:13) and where there was no work, knowledge, or wisdom (Eccles. 9:5–6, 10). The righteous dreaded *sheol* because there was no praise or presence of God there (Ps. 6:5), and deliverance from it is a blessing (Ps. 30:1–4). In Ezekiel, it is a land below, a place of reproach, and the abode of the uncircumcised (31:15–17).

Two Greek words stand behind the English word "hell" in the New Testament: *Hades* and *Gehenna.* The former was originally a proper noun, the name of the god of the underworld, and came to mean simply the underworld as the abode of the dead, a place in the depths in contrast to heaven (Matt. 11:23; Luke 10:15). It is personified in conjunction with death in Revelation 6:8 and elsewhere.

Gehenna was taken into Greek from a Hebrew expression that occurs in Joshua 15:8 and elsewhere meaning "the valley of the son of Hinnom," a ravine south of Jerusalem where, according to later Jewish popular belief, the final judgment was to be held. It may have been a smoking garbage dump for the city; its gloomy appearance suggested an appropriate setting for the wicked in the afterlife. Jesus spoke of hell fire (Matt. 5:22), of the damnation of hell (Matt. 23:33), and of a child of hell (Matt. 23:15).

MESSIANIC PROPHECY

Throughout the New Testament Gospel narratives, a refrain occurs again and again—"that the scripture might be fulfilled." Jesus himself spoke of the necessity of fulfilling the words of the Old Testament, with reference to his betrayal by Judas Iscariot (John 17:12). To the writers of those narratives, fulfillment of Old Testament prophecy was the proof *par excellence* of the authenticity of Jesus' messiahship, and even when they did not invoke the formula, "that the scripture might be fulfilled," their work is filled with allusions to the Old Testament. For example, when John the Baptist sent his disciples to inquire of Jesus if he were really the Messiah or whether they should look for another, the narrative reports that in that hour Jesus cured many of diseases, plagues, evil spirits, and blindness, and then told John's messengers to report to John what they had seen and heard, *viz.*, that these miracles were performed and that the poor had good news preached to them. "And blessed is he," Jesus added, "who takes no offense at me" (Luke 7:19–23 RSV). Although Luke makes no explicit mention of it, he fully expected that his readers would be familiar enough with Isaiah to recognize Jesus' allusions to portions of chapters 29, 35, and 61 of that book.

The following is a list of some of the more explicit passages in the New Testament in which the writers assert or imply that a certain Old Testament Scripture has been fulfilled. The list pairs the Old and New Testament references together, so that the student can conveniently make comparisons for purposes of descriptive analysis.

1. Gen. 49:10; Luke 1:32–33
2. Isa. 9:7; Luke 1:32–33
3. Mic. 5:2; Matt. 2:5–6
4. Isa. 7:14; Luke 1:26–35
5. Jer. 31:15; Matt. 2:16–18
6. Dan. 2:44; John 18:36 and 1 Cor. 15:24

7. Deut. 18:15; John 6:14
8. Isa. 53:1–12; John 1:11, 29
9. Isa. 11:2; Luke 2:52; 4:18
10. Zech. 9:9–10; John 12:13–15 and Matt. 21:4–5
11. Ps. 22:18; Matt. 27:35
12. Ps. 41:9; John 13:38
13. Ps. 69:21; Matt. 27:34
14. Zech. 11:12; Matt. 26:15
15. Zech. 12:10; John 19:34
16. Mal. 3:1–4; life of Christ in Gospels.
17. Hos. 11:1; Matt. 2:15
18. Isa. 40:3; Matt. 3:3 and John 1:23
19. Isa. 9:1–2; Matt. 4:14–16
20. Isa. 53:4; Matt. 8:17
21. Mic. 7:6; Matt. 10:35
22. Mal. 3:1; Matt. 11:10
23. Isa. 42:1–4; Matt. 12:18–21
24. Isa. 6:9–10; Matt. 13:14–15
25. Ps. 78:2; Matt. 13:35
26. Ps. 118:22–23; Matt. 21:42
27. Ps. 110:1; Matt. 22:43–44 (Acts 2:34–35)
28. Zech. 13:7; Matt. 26:31
29. Ps. 110:1 and Dan. 7:13; Matt. 26:64
30. Jer. 32:6–9; Matt. 27:9–10
31. Ps. 22:1; Matt. 27:46
32. Ps. 118:25–26; Mark 11:9
33. Isa. 13:10 and Ezek. 32:7–8; Mark 13:24–25
34. Ps. 78:24 (105:40); John 6:33–35
35. Ps. 16:8–11; Acts 2:25–28

Bibliography

Abbott, Walter M., and Rabbi Arthur Gilbert (eds.). *The Bible Reader*. New York: Bruce, 1969.

This book is a condensed Bible with a running commentary on some of the interesting passages. (The editors have selected what they feel are the most relevant parts of the Bible, leaving out such chapters as genealogies, etc.)

Albright, William Foxwell. *From the Stone Age to Christianity: Monotheism and the Historical Process*. 2d ed. Garden City, N.Y.: Doubleday, 1957.

Albright, in the above book, discusses the development of the religion of Israel, pointing out interesting facts about archaeological discoveries, etc.

Buttrick, George Arthur (ed.). *The Interpreter's Bible*. 12 vols. New York: Abingdon Press, 1952–1957.

This set of books deals with the entire Bible in a scholarly manner, giving various viewpoints on controversial issues which arise over most parts of the Bible. Amongst religious scholars, it is considered to be "liberal" in viewpoint.

Capps, Alton C. (ed.). *The Bible as Literature*. New York: McGraw-Hill, 1971.

This book is helpful to those who wish to study the various literary forms of the Bible. The editor has broken down the Bible into forms, selecting the most appropriate biblical passages to illustrate the given form.

169

Ellicott, Charles J. (ed.). *Ellicott's Commentary on the Whole Bible.* Grand Rapids, Michigan: Zondervan, 1961.

This commentary gives a scholarly, yet simple commentary on the entire Bible. Amongst religious scholars, it is considered to be "fundamental" or "traditional" in viewpoint.

Erskine, John. *The Human Life of Jesus.* New York: William Morrow, 1946.

This is an excellent book, which reads like a novel, and gives one an idea of what Jesus might have felt like, growing up as a man. It is conjecture, but conjecture based upon real geographical and historical background.

Freeman, James M. *Manners and Customs of the Bible.* Plainfield, New Jersey: Logos International, 1972.

A book explaining all the manners and customs that were common, everyday knowledge in Bible times, but which, over the ensuing twenty or more centuries, have become more and more obscure.

Gaster, Theodor H., *Myth, Legend, and Custom in the Old Testament.* New York: Harper & Row, 1969.

This book treats the stories of the Bible as myths, and parallels them with the myths of various civilizations, attempting to explain the reasons for their birth. For example, Gaster discusses the "mark of Cain" at length, bringing in every possible reason and explanation for such a mark. It is interesting reading, and certainly quite non-religious in viewpoint.

Goodspeed, Edgar J. *The Story of the New Testament.* Chicago: The University of Chicago Press, 1962.

Goodspeed is a renowned biblical scholar who writes in a clear, lucid style. The book is a classic in its field, shedding a great deal of light on the writing of the New Testament. One must bear in mind, of course, that the book contains Goodspeed's view of the writing of the New Testament, and like any other theory, his is open to challenge.

Guthrie, D., and J. A. Motyer (eds.). *The New Bible Commentary, Revised.* Grand Rapids, Michigan: Eerdmans, 1970.

This is a one-volume commentary, scholarly, brief, to the point, fundamental-traditional in view, and yet quite up-to-date in archaeological and other data related to biblical issues. It is an excellent quick source to consult, and provides an interesting contrast to *The Interpreter's Bible.*

Miller, H. S. *General Biblical Introduction.* New York: The Word-Bearer Press, 1960.

This is an excellent source on the canonization of the Bible. It is fundamental-traditional in view, and is a good contrast to *The Bible Reader,* which presents the "priestly" theory of canonization.

Morris, Henry M. et al. *A Symposium on Creation.* Grand Rapids, Michigan: Baker Book House, 1968.

For those who do not accept the theory of evolution without question, this is an excellent resource. It provides logical arguments, presented by learned men (mainly scientists), refuting the plausibility of the theory of evolution.

Stoner, Peter W., *Science Speaks,* Chicago: Moody Press, 1958.

This simply written book has as its goal to prove that the Bible is scientifically verifiable. Stoner presents countless examples of biblical claims which are proven in nature itself. This is interesting reading for anyone, religious or otherwise.

Tenney, Merrill C. (ed.). *Zondervan Pictorial Bible Dictionary.* Grand Rapids, Michigan: Zondervan, 1963.

If one were to have only one biblical reference book, this should be it. It contains reliable, scholarly information on every aspect of the Bible, from A to Z. It is the best job that could conceivably be done in one volume.

Viening, Edward (ed.). *The Zondervan Topical Bible.* Grand Rapids, Michigan: Zondervan, 1969.

This "Bible" is actually a simplified concordance. It takes any subject and gives the entire biblical reference scope for that reference, quoting the most relevant references and giving background information where relevant. This is a very helpful book when one wants to have a quick overview of a given topic, without thumbing through the entire Bible.

Vos, Howard F. (ed.). *Can I Trust the Bible?* Chicago: Moody Press, 1963.

This book's purpose is to prove that the Bible is an authentic book, historically, scientifically, spiritually, prophetically and in every respect. The authors vary in scholarship; some are learned and impressive, while others are simply zealous without scholarship. This is an excellent book for one who is interested in the validity of the Bible, and various views on the subject.

Vos, Howard F. *Genesis and Archaeology.* Chicago: Moody Press, 1963.

The author of this book gives numerous examples of archaeological excavations which have verified data in the book of Genesis.

Whitcomb, John C. and Morris, H.M. *The Genesis Flood.* Philadelphia: Presbyterian and Reformed Publishing Company, 1960.

A remarkable and somewhat technical treatment of the whole flood dispute that describes the different points of view. The authors argue earnestly for the literal interpretation.

Wight, Fred H. *Manners and Customs of Bible Lands.* Chicago: Moody Press, 1953.

This book gives valuable information about the geography, population, culture, customs, etc., of the Middle East from the days of Abraham through the days of Jesus. It helps one to better understand many passages of the Bible.

Concordances

A biblical concordance is an alphabetical listing of the principal words of the Bible with a reference to the passage in which each occurs and a phrase of the context. Many excellent and thorough concordances of the King James Version exist, the most famous of which was compiled by Alexander Cruden (1701–1770). Several editions of his work, abridged and unabridged, are in print today.

Book Report

The following books contain ideas which require a knowledge of the Bible. Select one (either a play or a novel) and write a book report, demonstrating how a knowledge of the Bible helped you to better understand the work.

Asch, S. *The Apostle* or *The Nazarene*
Bunyan, J. *Pilgrim's Progress*
Byatt, H. *The Testament of Judas*
Caldwell, T. *Dear and Glorious Physician,* or *Great Lion of God*
Costain, T. *The Silver Chalice*
Cronin, A. J. *The Keys to the Kingdom*
Dickens, C. *A Tale of Two Cities*
Douglas, L. *The Big Fisherman, The Robe*
Greene, G. *The Heart of the Matter,* or *The Power and the Glory*
Hardy, T. *Jude the Obscure*
Hawthorne, N. *The Scarlet Letter*
Jenkins, G. *King David*
Jenkins, S. *Song of Deborah*
Kazantzakis, N. *The Greek Passion, The Last Temptation of Christ*
Lee, H. *Inherit the Wind*
Mann, T. *Joseph in Egypt,* or *Joseph and His Brethren*
Marlowe, C. *Doctor Faustus*
Miller, A. *The Crucible*
Slaughter, F. *Upon This Rock*
Stowe, H. *Uncle Tom's Cabin*
Wallace, L. *Ben-Hur*

Waltari, M. *Secret of the Kingdom*
Uris, L. *Exodus*

There are also many interesting and informative non-fiction books related to the Bible. See the bibliography for many of them. Here are some not mentioned in the bibliography.

Cruz, N. *Run, Baby, Run*
Kagan, H. *Six Who Changed the World*
Muggeridge, H. *Jesus Revisited*
Nusabaum, M. *Away in a Manger*
Oursler, F. *The Greatest Story Ever Told*
Samuel, M. *Certain People of the Book*
Schaeffer, F. *The God Who Is There, Escape from Reason*
Schonfield, H. *The Passover Plot, The Bible Was Right*
Sherrill, J. *They Speak With Other Tongues*
Thompson, B. *Peter and Paul*
Wilkerson, D. *The Cross and the Switchblade*

Poetry Anthology

Contents

Amoretti. Sonnet lxviii

Most glorious Lord of life that on this day,
  didst make thy triumph over death and sin:
  and having harrowed hell, didst bring away
  captivity thence captive us to win:
This joyous day, dear Lord, with joy begin,
  and grant that we for whom thou diddest die
  being with thy dear blood clean washed from sin,
  may live for ever in felicity.
And that thy love we weighing worthily,
  may likewise love thee for the same again:
  and for thy sake that all like dear didst buy,
  with love may one another entertain.
So let us love, dear love, like as we ought,
  love is the lesson which the Lord us taught.

—Edmund Spenser

(Eph. 4:8; I John 1:7; John 13:34–35)

Sonnet CXLVI

Poor soul, the center of my sinful earth,
Thrall to these rebel powers that thee array,
Why dost thou pine within and suffer dearth,
Painting thy outward walls so costly gay?
Why so large cost, having so short a lease,
Dost thou upon thy fading mansion spend?
Shall worms, inheritors of this excess,
Eat up thy charge? Is this thy body's end?
Then, soul, live thou upon thy servant's loss,
And let that pine to aggravate thy store;
Buy terms divine in selling hours of dross;
Within be fed, without be rich no more:
  So shalt thou feed on Death, that feeds on men,
  And Death once dead, there's no more dying then.

—William Shakespeare

(Rom. 8:12–15; Matt. 16:26; Luke 12:16–21)

Holy Sonnet 1

Thou hast made me and shall thy work decay?
Repair me now, for now mine end doth haste,
I run to death and death meets me as fast,
And all my pleasures are like yesterday;
I dare not move my dim eyes any way,
Despair behind, and death before doth cast
Such terror, and my feeble flesh doth waste
By sin in it, which it towards hell doth weigh;
Only thou art above, and when towards thee
By thy leave I can look, I rise again;
But our old subtle foe so tempteth me,
That not one hour myself I can sustain;
Thy grace may wing me to prevent his art,
And thou like adamant draw mine iron heart.

—John Donne

(Rom. 6–8)

Holy Sonnet XIV

Batter my heart, three person'd God; for, you
As yet but knock, breathe, shine, and seek to mend;
That I may rise and stand, o'erthrow me, and bend
Your force, to break, blow, burn and make me new.
I, like an usurped town, to another due,
Labour to admit you, but O, to no end.
Reason, your viceroy in me, me should defend,
But is captiv'd, and proves weak or untrue.
Yet dearly I love you, and would be loved fain,
But am betroth'd unto your enemy:
Divorce me, untie, or break that knot again,
Take me to you, imprison me, for I
Except you enthrall me, never shall be free,
Nor ever chaste, except you ravish me.

—John Donne

(Rom. 7:24)

Bitter-Sweet

Ah, my dear angry Lord,
Since Thou dost love, yet strike;
Cast down, yet help afford;
Sure I will do the like.

I will complain, yet praise,
I will bewail, approve;
And all my sour-sweet days
I will lament, and love.

—George Herbert

(Heb. 12:3–11)

Love

Love bade me welcome; yet my soul drew back,
　Guilty of dust and sin.
But quick-eyed Love, observing me grow slack
　From my first entrance in,
Drew nearer to me, sweetly questioning
　If I lacked anything.

"A guest," I answered, "worthy to be here":
　Love said, "You shall be he."
"I, the unkind, ungrateful? Ah, my dear
　I cannot look on Thee."
Love took my hand, and smiling did reply,
　"Who made the eyes but I?"

"Truth, Lord; but I have marred them; let my shame
　Go where it doth deserve."
"And know you not," says Love, "who bore the blame?"
　"My dear, then I will serve."
"You must sit down," says Love, "and taste my meat."
　So I did sit and eat.

—George Herbert

(Luke 14:15–24; John 6:51–59)

Easter

Rise, heart, thy Lord is risen. Sing his praise
          Without delays,
Who takes thee by the hand, that thou likewise
          With him mayst rise;
That, as his death calcined thee to dust,
His life may make thee gold, and much more, just.

Awake, my lute, and struggle for thy part
          With all thy art:
The cross taught all wood to resound his name
          Who bore the same;
His stretched sinews taught all strings what key
Is best to celebrate this most high day.

Consort both heart and lute, and twist a song
          Pleasant and long.
Or, since all music is but three parts vied
          And multiplied,
O let thy blessed Spirit bear a part,
And make up our defects with his sweet art.

—George Herbert

(Rom. 5:10; 1 Cor. 15:20)

The Garden of Eden (from *Paradise Lost*)

Out of the fertile ground he caused to grow
All trees of noblest kind for sight, smell, taste;
And all amid them stood the Tree of Life,
High eminent, blooming ambrosial fruit
Of vegetable gold; and next to life,
Our death, the Tree of Knowledge, grew fast by—
Knowledge of good, bought dear by knowing ill.
Southward through Eden went a river large,
Nor changed his course, but through the shaggy hill
Passed underneath ingulfed; for God had thrown
That mountain, as his garden-mould, high raised
Upon the rapid current, which, through veins
Of porous earth with kindly thirst updrawn,
Rose a fresh fountain, and with many a rill
Watered the garden; thence united fell
Down the steep glade, and met the nether flood,
Which from his darksome passage now appears,
And now, divided into four main streams,
Runs diverse, wandering many a famous realm
And country whereof here needs no account;
But rather to tell how, if Art could tell
How, from the sapphire fount the crispèd brooks,
Rowling on orient Pearl and sands of Gold . . .

—John Milton

(Gen. 2:8–11)

Eve's Temptation (from *Paradise Lost*)

To Whom the Tempter guilefully replied:—
"Indeed! Hath God then said that of the fruit
Of all these garden-trees ye shall not eat,
Yet Lords declared of all in Earth and Air?"
    To whom thus Eve, yet sinless:—"Of the fruit
Of each tree in the garden we may eat;
But of the fruit of this fair Tree, amidst
The Garden, God hath said, 'Ye shall not eat
Thereof, nor shall ye touch it, lest ye die.' "

.   .   .   .

Why then was this forbid? Why but to awe,
Why but to keep ye low and ignorant,
His worshipers? He knows that in the day
Ye eat thereof your eyes, that seem so clear,
Yet are but dim, shall perfectly be then
Opened and cleared, and ye shall be as Gods,
Knowing both good and evil, as they know.

—John Milton

(Gen. 3:1–5)

The Flood (from *Paradise Lost*)

The Ark no more now floats, but seems on ground,
Fast on the top of some high mountain fixed.
And now the tops of hills as rocks appear;
With clamour thence the rapid currents drive
Towards the retreating sea their furious tide.
Forthwith from out the ark a Raven flies,
And, after him, the surer messenger,
A Dove, sent forth once and again to spy
Green tree or ground whereon his foot may light;
The second time returning, in his bill
An olive-leaf he brings, pacific sign.
Anon dry ground appears, and from his ark
The ancient sire descends with all his train;
Then, with uplifted hands and eyes devout,
Grateful to Heaven, over his head beholds
A dewy cloud, and in the cloud a Bow
Conspicuous with three listed colours gay,
Betokening peace from God, and covenant new.

—John Milton

(Gen. 8:3–11; 9:11–15)

Easter Hymn

Death and darkness get you packing,
Nothing now to man is lacking;
All your triumphs now are ended,
And what Adam marred is mended;
Graves are beds now for the weary,
Death a nap, to wake more merry;
Youth now, full of pious duty,
Seeks in thee for perfect beauty;
The weak and aged, tir'd with length
Of days, from thee look for new strength;
And infants with thy pangs contest
As pleasant, as if with the breast.
   Then, unto Him, who thus hath thrown
Even to contempt thy kingdom down,
And by His blood did us advance
Unto His own inheritance,
To Him be glory, power, praise,
From this, unto the last of days!

—Henry Vaughan

(Rom. 5:12–21; 1 Cor. 15:54–55)

'Mock on, Mock on, Voltaire, Rousseau'

Mock on, mock on, Voltaire, Rousseau;
Mock on, mock on; 'tis all in vain!
You throw the sand against the wind,
And the wind blows it back again.

And every sand becomes a gem
Reflected in the beams divine;
Blown back they blind the mocking eye,
But still in Israel's paths they shine.

The Atoms of Democritus
And Newton's Particles of Light
Are sands upon the Red Sea shore,
Where Israel's tents do shine so bright.

—William Blake

(Exod. 14)

Ode to a Nightingale

My heart aches, and a drowsy numbness pains
  My sense, as though of hemlock I had drunk,
Or emptied some dull opiate to the drains
  One minute past, and Lethe-wards had sunk:
'Tis not through envy of thy happy lot,
    But being too happy in thy happiness,—
      That thou, light winged Dryad of the trees,
        In some melodious plot
    Of beechen green, and shadows numberless,
      Singest of summer in full-throated ease.

O for a draught of vintage! that hath been
  Cool'd a long age in the deep-delvèd earth,
Tasting of Flora and the country-green,
  Dance, and Provençal song, and sunburnt mirth!
O for a beaker full of the warm South!
    Full of the true, the blushful Hippocrene,
      With beaded bubbles winking at the brim,
        And purple-stainèd mouth;
    That I might drink, and leave the world unseen,
      And with thee fade away into the forest dim:

Fade far away, dissolve, and quite forget
  What thou among the leaves hast never known,
The weariness, the fever, and the fret
  Here, where men sit and hear each other groan;
Where palsy shakes a few, sad, last gray hairs,
    Where youth grows pale, and specter-thin, and dies;
      Where but to think is to be full of sorrow
        And leaden-eyed despairs;
    Where Beauty cannot keep her lustrous eyes,
      Or new Love pine at them beyond to-morrow.

   .   .   .   .

Darkling I listen; and, for many a time
  I have been half in love with easeful Death,
Call'd him soft names in many a musèd rhyme,
  To take into the air my quiet breath;
Now more than ever seems it rich to die,
  To cease upon the midnight with no pain,
    While thou are pouring forth thy soul abroad
      In such an ecstasy!
  Still wouldst thou sing, and I have ears in vain—
    To thy high requiem become a sod.

Thou wast not born for death, immortal bird!
  No hungry generations tread thee down;
The voice I hear this passing night was heard
  In ancient days by emperor and clown:
Perhaps the self-same song that found a path
  Through the sad heart of Ruth, when, sick for home,
    She stood in tears amid the alien corn;
      The same that oft-times hath
  Charm'd the magic casements, opening on the foam
  Of perilous seas, in faery lands forlorn.

Forlorn! the very word is like a bell
  To toll me back from thee to my sole self!
Adieu! the fancy cannot cheat so well
  As she is famed to do, deceiving elf.
Adieu! adieu! thy plaintive anthem fades
  Past the near meadows, over the still stream,
    Up the hill-side; and now 'tis buried deep
      In the next valley-glades:
  Was it a vision, or a waking dream?
    Fled is that music:—do I wake or sleep?

—John Keats

(Ruth, especially 2:17)

God Our Refuge

If there had anywhere appeared in space
  Another place of refuge where to flee,
Our hearts had taken refuge in that place,
    And not with Thee.

For we against creation's bars had beat
  Like prisoned eagles, through great worlds had sought
Though but a foot of ground to plant our feet,
    Where Thou wert not.

And only when we found in earth and air,
  In heaven or hell, that such might nowhere be—
That we could not flee from Thee anywhere,
    We fled to Thee.

—Richard Chenevix Trench

(Ps. 139:7–8)

Crossing the Bar

Sunset and evening star,
  And one clear call for me!
And may there be no moaning of the bar,
  When I put out to sea,

But such a tide as moving seems asleep,
  Too full for sound and foam,
When that which drew from out the boundless deep
  Turns again home.

Twilight and evening bell,
  And after that the dark!
And may there be no sadness of farewell,
  When I embark;

For though from out our bourn of Time and Place
  The flood may bear me far,
I hope to see my Pilot face to face
  When I have crossed the bar.

                              —*Alfred, Lord Tennyson*

(1 Cor. 13:12)

" 'Remember me,' implored the Thief"

"Remember me," implored the Thief—
Oh magnanimity!
"My Visitor in Paradise
I give thee Guaranty."

That courtesy will fair remain,
When the delight is dust,
With which we cite this mightiest case
Of compensated Trust.

Of All, we are allowed to hope,
But Affadavit stands
That this was due, where some, we fear,
Are unexpected friends.

—Emily Dickinson

(Luke 23:39–43)

"At least to pray is left, is left"

At least to pray is left, is left.
O Jesus! in the air
I know not which thy chamber is,—
I'm knocking everywhere.

Thou stirrest earthquake in the South,
And maelstrom in the sea;
Say, Jesus Christ of Nazareth,
Hast thou no arm for me?

—Emily Dickinson

(Matt. 7:7–8; Ps. 88)

"I took my power in my hand"

I took my power in my hand
And went against the world;
'Twas not so much as David had,
But I was twice as bold.

I aimed my pebble, but myself
Was all the one that fell.
Was it Goliath was too large,
Or only I too small?

                    —*Emily Dickinson*

(I Sam. 17)

"My life closed twice before its close"

My life closed twice before its close;
    It yet remains to see
If Immortality unveil
    A third event to me,

So huge, so hopeless to conceive,
    As these that twice befell.
Parting is all we know of heaven,
    And all we need of hell.

                    —*Emily Dickinson*

(Luke 16:26)

In the Servants' Quarters

"Man, you too, aren't you, one of these rough followers of the
    criminal?
All hanging hereabout to gather how he's going to bear
Examination in the hall." She flung disdainful glances on
The shabby figure standing at the fire with the others there,
    Who warmed them by its flare.

"No indeed, my skipping maiden: I know nothing of the trial
    here,
Or criminal, if so he be. — I chanced to come this way,
And the fire shown out into the dawn, and morning airs are
    cold now;
I, too, was drawn by charms I see before me play,
    That I see not every day."

"Ha, ha!" then laughed the constables who also stood to warm
    themselves,
The while another maiden scrutinized his features hard,
As the blaze threw into contrast every line and knot that
    wrinkled them,
Exclaiming, "Why, last night when he was brought in by the
    guard,
    You were with him in the yard!"

"Nay, nay, you teasing wench, I say! You know you speak
    mistakenly,
Cannot a tired pedestrian who has legged it long and far
Here on his way from northern parts, engrossed in humble
    marketings,
Come in and rest awhile, although judicial doings are
    Afoot by morning star?"

"O, come, come!" laughed the constables. "Why, man, you
    speak the dialect
He uses in his answers; you can hear him up the stairs.

So own it. We sha'n't hurt ye. There he's speaking now! His
    syllables
Are those you sound yourself when you are talking unawares,
    As the pretty girl declares."

"And you shudder when his chain clinks!" she rejoined. "O yes,
    I noticed it.
And you winced, too, when those cuffs they gave him echoed to
    us here.
They'll soon be coming down, and you may then have to defend
    yourself
Unless you hold your tongue, or go away and keep you clear
    When he's led to judgment near!"

"No, I'll be damned in hell if I know anything about the man!
No single thing about him more than anybody knows.
Must not I even warm my hands but I am charged with blas-
    phemies?" . . .
— His face convulses as the morning cock that moment crows,
    And he droops, and turns, and goes.

— Thomas Hardy

(Matt. 26:69–75; Luke 22:54–62)

A Drizzling Easter Morning

And he is risen? Well, be it so. . . .
And still the pensive lands complain,
And dead men wait as long ago,
As if, much doubting, they would know
What they are ransomed from, before
They pass again their sheltering door.

I stand amid them in the rain,
While blusters vex the yew and vane;
And on the road the weary wain
Plods forward, laden heavily;
And toilers with their aches are fain
For endless rest—though risen is he.

—Thomas Hardy

(Heb. 2:8)

Thou art indeed just, Lord

Thou art indeed just, Lord, if I contend
With thee; but, sir, so what I plead is just.
Why do sinners' ways prosper? and why must
Disappointment all I endeavour end?
   Wert thou mine enemy, O thou my friend,
How wouldst thou worst, I wonder, than thou dost
Defeat, thwart me? Oh, the sots and thralls of lust
Do in spare hours more thrive than I that spend,
Sir, life upon thy cause. See, banks and brakes
Now, leavèd how thick! lacèd they are again
With fretty chervil, look, and fresh wind shakes
Them; birds build—but not I build; no, but strain,
Time's eunuch, and not breed one work that wakes.
Mine, O thou lord of life, send my roots rain.

                       —*Gerard Manley Hopkins*
(Ps. 73)

In the Valley of the Elwy

I remember a house where all were good
   To me, God knows, deserving no such thing:
   Comforting smell breathed at very entering,
Fetched fresh, as I suppose, off some sweet wood.
That cordial air made those kind people a hood
   All over, as a bevy of eggs the mothering wing
   Will, or mild nights the new morsels of spring:
Why, it seemed of course; seemed of right it should.

Lovely the woods, waters, meadows, combes, vales,
All the air things wear that build this world of Wales;
   Only the inmate does not correspond:
God, lover of souls, swaying considerate scales,
Complete thy creature dear O where it fails,
   Being mighty a master, being a father and fond.

                       —*Gerard Manley Hopkins*
(Rom. 7:21–24)

Christ in the Universe

With this ambiguous earth
His dealings have been told us. These abide:
The signal to a maid, the human birth,
The lesson, and the young Man crucified.

But not a star of all
The innumerable hosts of stars has heard
How He administered this terrestrial ball.
Our race have kept their Lord's entrusted Word.

Of His earth-visiting feet
None knows the secret, cherished, perilous,
The terrible, shamefast, frightened, whispered, sweet,
Heart-shattering secret of His way with us.

No planet knows of this.
Our wayside planet, carrying land and wave,
Love and life multiplied, and pain and bliss,
Bears, as chief treasure, one forsaken grave.

Nor, in our little day,
May His devices with the heavens be guessed;
His pilgrimage to thread the Milky Way,
Or His bestowals there, be manifest.

But, in the eternities,
Doubtless we shall compare together, hear
A million alien Gospels, in what guise
He trod the Pleiades, the Lyre, the Bear.

O be prepared, my soul!
To read the inconceivable, to scan
The myriad forms of God those stars unroll
When, in our turn, we show to them a Man.

                                        — *Alice Meynell*

(Luke 1:26–38; 2:1–7; Mark 16:25)

E Tenebris

Come down, O Christ, and help me! reach thy hand,
  For I am drowning in a stormier sea
  Than Simon on thy lake of Galilee:
The wine of life is spilt upon the sand,
My heart is in some famine-murdered land
  Whence all good things have perished utterly,
  And well I know my soul in Hell must lie
If I this night before God's throne should stand.
"He sleeps perchance, or rideth to the chase,
  Like Baal, when his prophets howled that name
  From morn to noon on Carmel's smitten height."
Nay, peace, I shall behold, before the night,
  The feet of brass, the robe more white than flame,
The wounded hands, the weary human face.

—Oscar Wilde

(I Kings 18:20–29; Matt. 14:22–30; Rev. 1:14–15)

The Carpenter's Son

'Here the hangman stops his cart:
Now the best of friends must part.
Fare you well, for ill fare I:
Live, lads, and I will die.

'Oh, at home had I but stayed
'Prenticed to my father's trade,
Had I stuck to plane and adze,
I had not been lost, my lads.

'Then I might have built perhaps
Gallows-trees for other chaps,
Never dangled on my own,
Had I but left ill alone.

'Now, you see, they hang me high,
And the people passing by
Stop to shake their fists and curse;
So 'tis come from ill to worse.

'Here hang I, and right and left
Two poor fellows hang for theft:
All the same's the luck we prove,
Though the midmost hangs for love.

'Comrades all, that stand and gaze,
Walk henceforth in other ways;
See my neck and save your own:
Comrades all, leave ill alone.

'Make some day a decent end,
Shrewder fellows than your friend.
Fare you well, for ill fare I:
Live, lads, and I will die.'

                                                        —*A. E. Housman*

(Mark 15:29–32)

Easter Hymn

If in that Syrian garden, ages slain,
You sleep, and know not you are dead in vain,
Nor even in dreams behold how dark and bright
Ascends in smoke and fire by day and night
The hate you died to quench and could but fan,
Sleep well and see no morning, son of man.

But if, the grave rent and the stone rolled by,
At the right hand of majesty on high
You sit, and sitting so remember yet
Your tears, your agony and bloody sweat,
Your cross and passion and the life you gave,
Bow hither out of heaven and see and save.

—A. E. Housman

(John 19:41–42; Heb. 1:1–4)

The Magi

Now as at all times I can see in the mind's eye,
In their stiff, painted clothes, the pale unsatisfied ones
Appear and disappear in the blue depth of the sky
With all their ancient faces like rain-beaten stones,
And all their helms of silver hovering side by side,
And all their eyes still fixed, hoping to find once more.
Being by Calvary's turbulence unsatisfied,
The uncontrollable mystery on the bestial floor.

—W. B. Yeats

(Matt. 2:1–12)

Ecclesiastes

There is one sin: to call a green leaf grey,
　　Whereat the sun in heaven shuddereth.
There is one blasphemy: for death to pray,
　　For God alone knoweth the praise of death.

There is one creed: 'neath no world-terror's wing
　　Apples forget to grow on apple-trees.
There is one thing is needful — everything —
　　The rest is vanity of vanities.

— G. K. Chesterton

(Ps. 88:10–12; Luke 10:42; Eccles. 1:2)

Bereft

Where had I heard this wind before
Change like this to a deeper roar?
What would it take my standing there for,
Holding open a restive door,
Looking down hill to a frothy shore?
Summer was past and day was past.
Somber clouds in the west were massed.
Out on the porch's sagging floor
Leaves got up in a coil and hissed,
Blindly struck at my knee and missed.
Something sinister in the tone
Told me my secret must be known:
Word I was in the house alone
Somehow must have gotten abroad,
Word I was in my life alone,
Word I had no one left but God.

— Robert Frost

(Ps. 73:25)

Ballad of the Goodly Fere

Simon Zelotes speaketh it somewhile
after the Crucifixion

Ha' we lost the goodliest fere o' all
For the priests and the gallows tree?
Aye lover he was of brawny men,
O' ships and the open sea.

When they came wi' a host to take Our Man
His smile was good to see;
"First let these go!" quo' our Goodly Fere,
"Or I'll see ye damned," says he.

Aye, he sent us out through the crossed high spears,
And the scorn of his laugh rang free;
"Why took ye not me when I walked about
Alone in the town?" says he.

Oh, we drunk his "Hale" in the good red wine
When we last made company;
No capon priest was the Goodly Fere
But a man o' men was he.

I ha' seen him drive a hundred men
Wi' a bundle o' cords swung free,
That they took the high and holy house
For their pawn and treasury.

They'll no' get him a' in a book I think,
Though they write it cunningly;
No mouse of the scrolls was the Goodly Fere
But aye loved the open sea.

If they think they ha' snared our Goodly Fere
They are fools to the last degree.
"I'll go to the feast," quo' our Goodly Fere,
"Though I go to the gallows tree."

"Ye ha' seen me heal the lame and blind,
And wake the dead," says he;
"Ye shall see one thing to master all:
'Tis how a brave man dies on the tree."

A Son of God was the Goodly Fere
That bade us his brothers be.
I ha' seen him cow a thousand men.
I have seen him upon the tree.

He cried no cry when they drave the nails
And the blood gushed hot and free;
The hounds of the crimson sky gave tongue
But never a cry cried he.

I ha' seen him cow a thousand men
On the hills o' Galilee;
They whined as he walked out calm between,
Wi' his eyes like the grey o' the sea.

Like the sea that brooks no voyaging
With the winds unleashed and free,
Like the sea that he cowed at Genseret
Wi' twey words spoke' suddenly.

A master of men was the Goodly Fere,
A mate of the wind and sea;
If they think they ha' slain our Goodly Fere
They are fools eternally.

I ha' seen him eat o' the honey-comb
Sin' they nailed him to the tree.

—*Ezra Pound*

(Luke 22:52–53; John 2:13–17; Luke 18:31–34;
Matt. 15:30–31; John 10:31–39)

Babylon

Babylon that was beautiful is Nothing now.
Once to the world it tolled a golden bell:
Belshazzar wore its blaze upon his brow;
Ruled; and to ruin fell.
Babylon — a blurred and blinded face of stone —
At dumb Oblivion bragged with trumpets blown;
Teemed, and while merchants throve and prophets dreamed,
Bowed before idols, and was overthrown.

Babylon the merciless, now a name of doom,
Built towers in Time, as we today, for whom
Auguries of self-annihilation loom.

—Siegfried Sassoon

(Jer. 50–51; Dan. 5; Rev. 14:8)

Noah

When old Noah stared across the floods,
Sky and water melted into one
Looking glass of shifting tides and sun.

Mountain-tops were few: the ship was foul:
All the morn old Noah marvelled greatly
At this weltering world that shone so stately,
Drowning deep the rivers and the plains.
Through the stillness came a rippling breeze;
Noah sighed, remembering the green trees.
Clear along the morning stooped a bird,
Lit beside him with a blossomed sprig.
Earth was saved; and Noah danced a jig.

—Siegfried Sassoon

(Gen. 6:9–8:22)

The End of the World

Quite unexpectedly as Vasserot
The armless ambidextrian was lighting
A match between his great and second toe
And Ralph the lion was engaged in biting
The neck of Madame Sossman while the drum
Pointed, and Teeny was about to cough
In waltz-time swinging Jocko by the thumb—
Quite unexpectedly the top blew off:

And there, there overhead, there, there, hung over
Those thousands of white faces, those dazed eyes,
There in the starless dark the poise, the hover,
There with vast wings across the canceled skies,
There in the sudden blackness the black pall
Of nothing, nothing, nothing—nothing at all.

—*Archibald MacLeish*

(Rev. 6:14)

The Maid-Servant at the Inn

"It's queer," she said; "I see the light
   As plain as I beheld it then,
All silver-like and calm and bright—
   We've not had stars like that again!

"And she was such a gentle thing
   To birth a baby in the cold.
The barn was dark and frightening—
   This new one's better than the old.

"I mind my eyes were full of tears,
   For I was young, and quick distressed,
But she was less than me in years
   That held a son against her breast.

"I never saw a sweeter child—
   The little one, the darling one!—
I mind I told her, when he smiled
   You'd know he was his mother's son.

"It's queer that I should see them so—
   The time they came to Bethlehem
Was more than thirty years ago;
   I've prayed that all is well with them."

              —*Dorothy Parker*

(Matt. 2:2; Luke 2:7)

At a Calvary Near the Ancre

One ever hangs where shelled roads part.
  In this war He too lost a limb,
But His disciples hide apart;
  And now the Soldiers bear with Him.

Near Golgotha strolls many a priest,
  And in their faces there is pride
That they were flesh-marked by the Beast
  By whom the gentle Christ's denied.

The scribes on all the people shove
  And brawl allegiance to the state,
But they who love the greater love
  Lay down their life; they do not hate.

—Wilfred Owen

(Luke 23:1–47)

The Parable of the Old Man and the Young

So Abram rose, and clave the wood, and went,
And took the fire with him, and a knife.
And as they sojourned both of them together,
Isaac the first-born spake and said, My Father,
Behold the preparations, fire and iron,
But where the lamb for this burnt-offering?
Then Abram bound the youth with belts and straps,
And builded parapets and trenches there,
And stretched forth the knife to slay his son.
When lo! an angel called him out of heaven,
Saying, Lay not thy hand upon the lad,
Neither do anything to him. Behold,
A ram caught in a thicket by its horns;
Offer the Ram of Pride instead of him.
But the old man would not so, but slew his son,
And half the seed of Europe, one by one.

—Wilfred Owen

(Gen. 22:1–14)

Divine Justice

God in His mercy made
The fixed pains of Hell.
That misery might be stayed,
God in His mercy made
Eternal bounds and bade
Its waves no further swell.
God in His mercy made
The fixed pains of Hell.

—C. S. Lewis

(Job 38:8–11)

The Nativity

Among the oxen (like an ox I'm slow)
I see a glory in the stable grow
Which, with an ox's dullness might at length
    Give me an ox's strength.

Among the asses (stubborn I as they)
I see my Saviour where I looked for hay;
So may my beastlike folly learn at least
    The patience of a beast.

Among the sheep (I like a sheep have strayed)
I watch the manger where my Lord is laid;
Oh that my baa-ing nature would win thence
    Some woolly innocence!

—C. S. Lewis

(Isa. 53:6)

Stephen to Lazarus

But was I the first martyr, who
Gave up no more than life, while you,
Already free among the dead,
Your rags stripped off, your fetters shed,
Surrendered what all other men
Irrevocably keep, and when
Your battered ship at anchor lay
Seemingly safe in the dark bay
No ripple stirs, obediently
Put out a second time to sea
Well knowing that your death (in vain
Died once) must all be died again?

—C. S. Lewis

(John 11:1–44; Acts 6:8–7:60)

Simon the Cyrenian Speaks

He never spoke a word to me,
  And yet He called my name;
He never gave a sign to me,
  And yet I knew and came.

At first I said, "I will not bear
  His cross upon my back;
He only seeks to place it there
  Because my skin is black."

But He was dying for a dream,
  And He was very meek,
And in His eyes there shone a gleam
  Men journey far to seek.

It was Himself my pity bought;
  I did for Christ alone
What all of Rome could not have wrought
  With bruise of lash or stone.

                                        —*Countee Cullen*

(Matt. 27:32)

The Litany of the Dark People

Our flesh that was a battle-ground
Shows now the morning-break;
The ancient deities are drowned
For thy eternal sake.
Now that the past is left behind,
Fling wide thy garment's hem
To keep us one with Thee in mind,
Thou Christ of Bethlehem.

The thorny wreath may ridge our brow,
The spear may mar our side,
And on white wood from a scented bough
We may be crucified;
Yet no assaults the old gods make
Upon our agony
Shall swerve our footsteps from the wake
Of Thine toward Calvary.

And if we hunger now and thirst,
Grant our withholders may,
When heaven's constellations burst
Upon Thy crowning day,
Be fed by us, and given to see
Thy mercy in our eyes,
When Bethlehem and Calvary
Are merged in Paradise.

—Countee Cullen

(John 19:1–37)

Seven Stanzas at Easter

Make no mistake: if He rose at all
it was as His body;
if the cells' dissolution did not reverse, the molecules
    reknit, the amino acids rekindle,
The Church will fall.

It was not as the flowers,
each soft Spring recurrent;
it was not as His Spirit in the mouths and fuddled
    eyes of the eleven apostles;
it was as His flesh: ours.

The same hinged thumbs and toes,
the same valved heart
that — pierced — died, withered, paused, and then
    regathered out of enduring Might
new strength to enclose.

Let us not mock God with metaphor,
analogy, sidestepping, transcendence;
making of the event a parable, a sign painted in the
    faded credulity of earlier ages:
let us walk through the door.

The stone is rolled back, not papier-mâché,
not a stone in a story,
but the vast rock of materiality that in the slow
    grinding of time will eclipse for each of us
the wide light of day.

And if we will have an angel at the tomb,
make it a real angel,
weighty with Max Planck's quanta, vivid with hair,
    opaque in the dawn light, robed in real linen
spun on a definite loom.

Let us not seek to make it less monstrous
for our own convenience, our own sense of beauty,
lest, awakened in one unthinkable hour, we are
   embarrassed by the miracle,
and crushed by remonstrance.

                                   —John Updike

(Matt. 28:1–7)

For Further Reading

Oxford Book of Christian Verse. ed. Lord David Cecil. Oxford, at the Clarendon Press, 1940.

Oxford Book of English Mystical Verse. Chosen by D. H. S. Nicholson and A. H. E. Lee. Oxford, at the Clarendon Press, 1917.

The World's Great Catholic Poetry. ed. Thomas Walsh. The Macmillan Co. 1947.

The Penguin Book of Religious Verse. Introduced and edited by R. S. Thomas. Penguin Books 1963.

The Harper Book of Christian Poetry. ed. by Anthony S. Mercatante. Harper and Row 1972.

General Index

Aaron, 46, 47, 48
Abdon, 52
Abednego, 89
Abel, 34
Abimelech, Judge of Israel, 52
Abraham (Abram), 24, 30, 38, 39, 40, 41, 47, 50, 107, 115, 118, 126, 132; call of, 36; faith of, 37
Abram, *see* Abraham
Absalom, Absalom, novel by William Faulkner, xix.
Achan, 51
acrostic, use of in Hebrew poetry, 70–71, 76; in Lamentations of Jeremiah, 86
Acts of the Apostles, The, 6, 19, 22, 115, 118, 139; discussion of, 122–24
Adam, 20, 30, 31, 33, 115, 118, 126
Additions to the Book of Esther, The, 16
Adriatic Sea, 139
Aegean Sea, 127, 149
Ahab, 61, 63–64
Ahasuerus, 69
Ai, 51
Albania, 139
Algeria, 40
Allenby, General, 156

Alexander the Great, 17, 24, 88
Amalekites, 58
Ammon, 87
Amos, Book of, 19, 21, 81; discussion of, 92–93; the prophet, 96
Anak, 57
Ananias, 123
Anointing, the practice of, 59
Antioch, 122, 139
anti-Semitism, 155
Apocalypse, *see also* Revelation, 6, 20
apocalyptic symbolism, examples of, 149
Apocrypha, 25; discussion of, 15–17
Apsu, Babylonian god of fresh water, 33
Ark of the Covenant, 56, 60, 62, 151
Arnold Matthew, *Culture and Anarchy,* 57
Asaph, sons of, 75
ascension of Jesus, 122
Ashdod, 57
Ashkelon, 57
Ashtoreth, 57
Ashur, city in Assyrian Empire, 97
Ashurbanipal, 96

217

Index of Biblical Passages

OLD TESTAMENT

NEW TESTAMENT